Jesus Invites You...

To the Marriage Supper of the Lamb

JESUS INVITES YOU... TO THE MARRIAGE SUPPER OF THE LAMB
by Jane C. Wittbold

Copyright © 2012-2019 Jane C. Wittbold
All rights reserved.

Published by:
RPJ & COMPANY, INC.
www.rpjandco.com
Orlando, Florida, U.S.A.

All rights reserved. No part of this book may be reproduced or transmitted in any form or by any means, electronic or mechanical, including photocopying, recording, or by any information storage and retrieval system, without written permission from the author, except for the inclusion of brief quotations in a review. For information, please contact the publisher.

ISBN-13: 978-1-937770-64-8

Excerpts taken from *God's Appointed Times* by Barney Kasdan, copyright ©1993, and *The Sabbath: Entering God's Rest* by Barry Rubin and Steffi Rubin, copyright ©1998. All rights reserved. Used by permission of Messianic Jewish Publishers. www.messianicjewish.net.

Cover & Interior Design by Kathleen Schubitz
RPJ & COMPANY, INC. | www.rpjandco.com

Cover Illustration:
Vintage background © Dmitry Skvorcov - Fotolia.com

Scripture verses are from the King James Version of the Bible, unless otherwise noted. All rights reserved.

Printed in the United States of America.

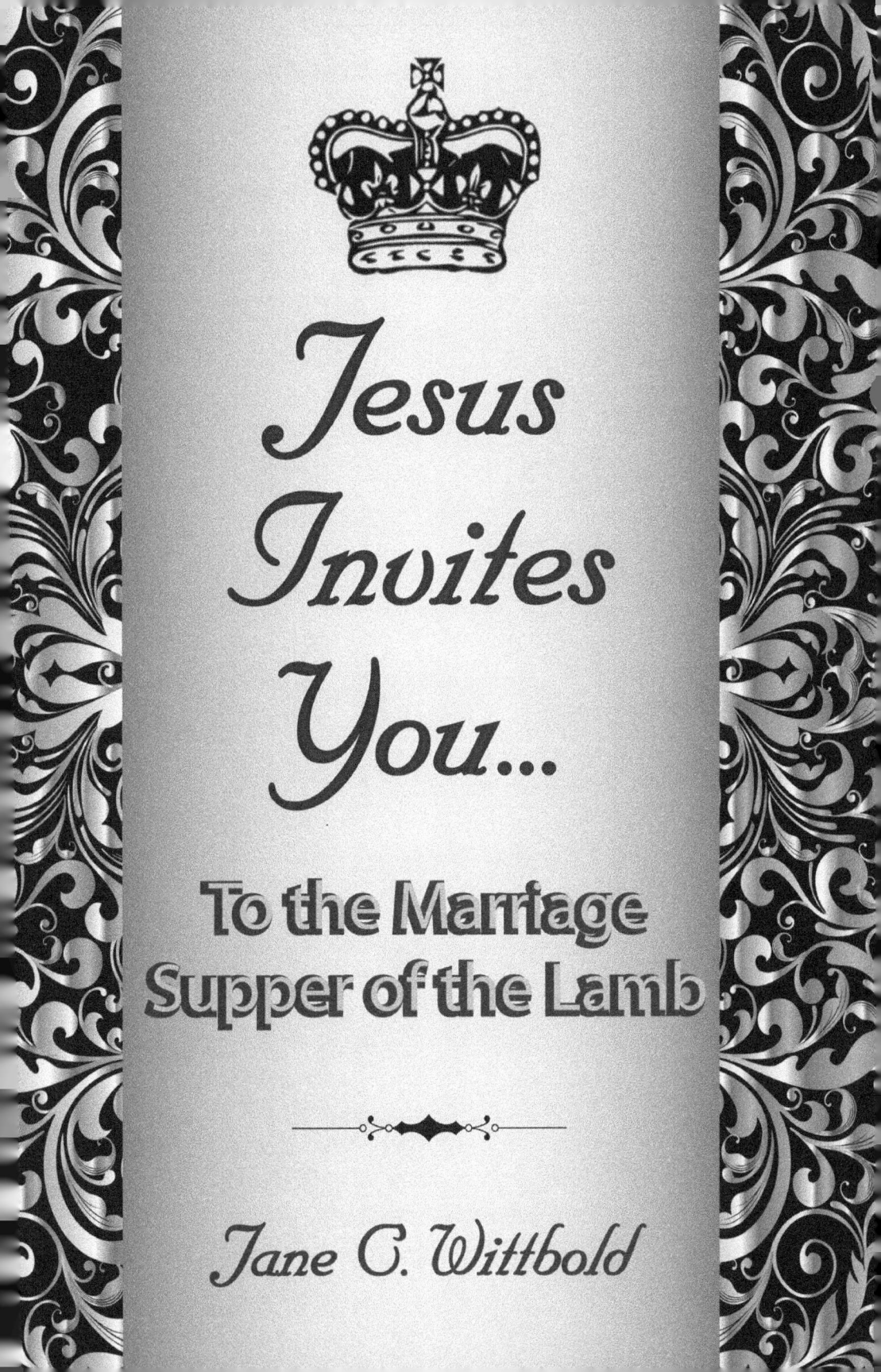

Revelation 19:7-9 *"Let us be glad and rejoice, and give honour to him: for the marriage of the Lamb is come, and his wife hath made herself ready. And to her was granted that she should be arrayed in fine linen, clean and white: for the fine linen is the righteousness of saints. And he saith unto me, Write, Blessed are they which are called unto the marriage supper of the Lamb. And he saith unto me, These are the true sayings of God."*

Revelation 22:17-21 *"And the Spirit and the bride say, Come. And let him that heareth say, Come. And let him that is athirst come. And whosoever will, let him take the water of life freely. For I testify unto every man that heareth the words of the prophecy of this book, If any man shall add unto these things, God shall add unto him the plagues that are written in this book: And if any man shall take away from the words of the book of this prophecy, God shall take away his part out of the book of life, and out of the holy city, and from the things which are written in this book. He which testifieth these things saith, Surely I come quickly. Amen. Even so, come, Lord Jesus. The grace of our Lord Jesus Christ be with you all. Amen.*

Published by:

RPJ & COMPANY, INC.
www.rpjandco.com

Table of Contents

Acknowledgments. IX

Dedication. xi

God's Call to Write 19

The Sins of our Fathers 27

Ancient Jewish Weddings 39

Introduction of the Hebrew Children 55

God Has a Plan 59

The Battle is Joined 67

The Departure from Egypt. 81

The Travel unto Sinai 85

God Prepared His People and They Became His Bride 93

An Overview of God's
Appointed Times and Holy Convocations 105

Shabbat, the Sabbath 111

God's Appointed Times, Fulfilled 116

Pesach, the Feast of Passover 117
    The Present Day Preparation of the Seder, the Meal of Order . . . 120
    The Seder Meal. 123
    Hag Ha Matzah, the Feast of Unleavened Bread 133
    The Omer, the time between Passover and Pentecost. 135
    Sfirat Haomar – Early First Fruits 138

Shavuot – Latter First Fruits, Pentecost 143

God's Appointed Times, Unfulfilled 148

Rosh HaShanah, the Feast of Trumpets 149
   Rosh HaShanah at the Temple and Synagogue Worship 152

Yom Kippur, the Day of Atonement 157
Yom Kippur Celebrations During the Temple Years 158
After the Destruction of the Temple..... 164

Sukkot, the Feast of Tabernacles 164

The Summation. 183

The Final Chapter 187

Personal Invitation 191

Resources 195

About the Author 196

Acknowledgments

I pray that God will send into the life of each devoted Christian someone who is knowledgeable and willing to share his or her great love of Israel, for there is no finer gift. For me that person was Jamie Buckingham and for many years we were a part of his flock in Melbourne Florida. Jamie named his church "The Tabernacle", and if you recall, that was the name of the original worship structure that God designed for His Hebrew children. It was planned by God and constructed under His personal supervision. The Hebrews used this Tabernacle regularly as they walked through the desolate places on the long and difficult journey to the Promised Land.

Though Jamie named his church "The Tabernacle", we lovingly called it "the Tab", and in pure Jamie speak, he often described his church as a "sheep shed". He commented that after some dipping, the bleating could be heard all over town.

Jamie planted seeds of joy into our hearts as he shared his great love for the land of Israel, and once we visited, we were overwhelmed with love.

A hard moment shook my life when my beloved Bill departed this coil and my consolation became God's message, *"Precious in the sight of the Lord is the death of his saints" (Psalm 116:15).*

In His perfect time, God blessed me with a return to the beloved land of Israel. Joining me in travel were faithful friends, those who had come to bear with me the burdens of the ministry that my husband and I had so diligently planted. I also want to thank the best guide in all of Israel, George Horesh, who shared his wisdom and knowledge of the land with us.

May the true heart of the Lord become yours as you read this book about the Hebrew people and their beloved Jehovah, the God of Israel. I hope that you accept and understand that I am not a teacher as much as I am a student, so forgive any errors, then study and rejoice with me.

Jane

Dedication

In answer to the question posed by the Lord, "To whom would you dedicate this book?" The answer was simple. Moses. After all, he was God's very best friend. Having spent the last few years studying him as he worked for God… first as servant, then friend, and finally as God's groomsman… I have come to appreciate and love him as God did. He was faithful to follow God and he was obedient to do almost everything that the Lord God asked of him, no matter how trying or difficult. It is interesting to hear what God said about him. *"(Now the man Moses was very meek, above all the men who were upon the face of the earth.)" (Numbers 12:3). And again He said, "With him will I speak, mouth to mouth, even apparently, and not in dark speeches; and the similitude of the Lord shall he behold:" (Numbers 12:8a).*

How awesome that a mere man so pleased God that he could share such a close relationship with Him. Moses kept it quiet. Everyone else knew, but Moses did not talk about it. It was God who disclosed it and made public this treasured relationship. It was God who announced His love for Moses. However there was one stain. It was at the waters of Meribah. *"And the LORD spake unto Moses, saying, Take the rod, and gather thou the assembly together, thou, and Aaron thy brother, and speak ye unto the rock before their eyes; and it shall give forth his water, and thou shalt bring forth to them water out of the rock: so thou shalt give the congregation and their beasts drink. And Moses took the rod from before the LORD, as he commanded him. And Moses and Aaron gathered the congregation together before the rock, and he said unto them, Hear now, ye rebels; must we fetch you water out of this rock? And Moses lifted up his hand, and with his rod he smote the rock twice: and the water came out abundantly, and the congregation drank, and their beasts also. And the LORD spake unto Moses and Aaron, Because ye believed me not, to sanctify me in the eyes of the children of Israel, therefore ye shall not bring this congregation into the land which I have given them" (Numbers 20:7-12).*

To me this is terribly sad. Though Moses had honored God through so much trial and trouble, his frustration with the Hebrew people betrayed him in that single moment and it cost him the crossing into the Promised Land. How many of us have moments like that? As we age we learn that they will always cost us something.

On my last trip to Israel we found we had a few extra days and George, my faithful guide, suggested that we spend them in the land of Jordan. After some thought I realized that though I had never really desired to travel in that part of the world, I now really wanted to stand where Moses stood, and hungered to see the Promised Land as he saw it. So along with my dear college friend, Dee Blakemore, we crossed from Israel to Jordan on the Allenby Bridge. Many had told us that it was nearly impossible to see the view as clearly as Moses had seen it since years of sand, heat and wind had destroyed the clarity of the air and few have seen it clearly since that time. It took some travel but we finally climbed that last hill and we indeed stood on that spot where Moses had once stood. When reading the scriptures about that time, see what God said unto Moses. *"Get thee up into this mountain Abarim, unto mount Nebo, which is in the land of Moab, that is over against Jericho; and behold the land of Canaan, which I give unto the children of Israel for a possession: And die in the mount whither thou goest up, and be gathered unto thy people; as Aaron thy brother died in mount Hor, and was gathered unto his people: Because ye trespassed against me among the children of Israel at the waters of Meribah-Kadesh, in the wilderness of Zin; because ye sanctified me not in the midst of the children of Israel. Yet thou shalt see the land before thee; but thou shalt not go thither unto the land which I give the children of Israel" (Deuteronomy 32:49-52).*

Then read as Moses responds to God. *"And Moses went up from the plains of Moab unto the mountain of Nebo, to the top of Pisgah, that is over against Jericho. And the LORD shewed him all the land of Gilead, unto Dan, And all Naphtali, and the land of Ephraim, and Manasseh, and all the land of Judah, unto the utmost sea, And the south, and the plain of the valley of Jericho, the city of palm trees, unto Zoar. And the LORD said unto him, This is the land which I sware unto Abraham, unto Isaac, and unto Jacob, saying, I will give it unto thy seed: I have caused thee to see it with thine eyes, but thou shalt not go over thither. So Moses the servant of the LORD died there in the land of Moab, according to the word of the LORD. And he buried him in a valley in the land of Moab, over against Bethpeor: but no man knoweth of his sepulchre unto this day. And Moses was an hundred and twenty years old when he died: his eye was not dim, nor his natural force abated. And the children of Israel wept for Moses in the plains of Moab thirty days: so the days of weeping and mourning for Moses were ended"* (Deuteronomy 34:1-8).

It is hard to miss the importance of this place and the view was wonderfully clear that day. I saw the palm trees of Jericho, and in the far distance the mountains that stood around Jerusalem. I saw mountains to the north, which I learned were the Benjamin Mountains and the beginning of the hill country of Ephraim. Far off to the south were the Judean foothills. It was wonderful. My eyes were not as clear as his, but I saw with joy some of that which Moses had seen. There were also the remains of an old synagogue that had once stood there to honor Moses. The ancient floor was covered with wonderful mosaics, which gave evidence that Moses had been there.

We also saw a sign that led to the so-called baptismal site of Jesus. No one knows for sure but this is said to be the location where John the Baptist did some of his ministry. The maps at the back of most Bibles will reveal that this was once a part of Israel.

It was added by King Saul and then increased under the kingdoms of both David and Solomon.

For those interested and planning to visit this part of the world, be sure to ask the guide to take you to the place that is called the Gadarenes in the Bible. It can be found in the beginning of the fifth chapter of Mark. It is just a short drive from Moses' location. Most people will remember the story this way. *"And when he was come to the other side into the country of the Gergesenes, there met him two possessed with devils, coming out of the tombs, exceeding fierce, so that no man might pass by that way. And, behold, they cried out, saying, What have we to do with thee, Jesus, thou Son of God? art thou come hither to torment us before the time? And there was a good way off from them an herd of many swine feeding. So the devils besought him, saying, If thou cast us out, suffer us to go away into the herd of swine. And he said unto them, Go. And when they were come out, they went into the herd of swine: and, behold, the whole herd of swine ran violently down a steep place into the sea, and perished in the waters. And they that kept them fled, and went their ways into the city, and told every thing, and what was befallen to the possessed of the devils. And, behold, the whole city came out to meet Jesus: and when they saw him, they besought him that he would depart out of their coasts"* (Matthew 8:28-34).

When first reading this verse, one may ask why in this story, were Jews keeping pigs? This was strictly forbidden and totally non-Kosher. For anyone who walks the area they will come to understand that though this was once Israel it became territory which was controlled by the Romans and Greeks, and a multitude of pagans still lived among the population when Jesus walked in that area. This is one of the true values of traveling in the area.

My dear child,

I will bless those of you who will read this book. I asked my daughter to write it for you because I wanted to teach you more about My chosen people and more about My ways.

The earthly time for the church is drawing to a close. It is important to pay close attention to what is happening in the heavenlies as well as on the earth. Jesus yearns for you to be here with Him, so I tell you the time is near. Study to show yourselves approved, then prepare yourselves to become the true bride of My beloved Son. I love you and honor those who will read this book.

Your Father

Jesus Invites You...

To the Marriage Supper of the Lamb

God's Call to Write

*T*hough writing is far from my favorite thing to do, there are good reasons for spending the day with your computer though a wonderful day beckons outside; the single and most important reason I know is that the Lord required it. He wanted me to write this book in order to help those who feel their relationship with Him is lacking something. It is also for those who hunger to fill that hollow place that lives within the very center of their being.

For those who are born again, yet lack the closeness with the Lord, then allow me to teach you that God has a really special gift for every reader. If we will allow Him, He will release Himself fully to us. It matters not your status — maiden, wife, husband or widow. He has this great gift for all of us. To borrow from Paul in his letter to the Galatians… Jew and Greek, bond and free, male and female, He would give Himself to us all in the role of a loving husband.

A while back, I wrote a book entitled, *Amazing Grace for Widows.* In the very midst of my husband's memorial service God spoke to me and made this promise: though Bill had been a wonderful husband, He, Jesus would be a better one. My job was to believe Him and make room in my heart for Him in order that He could become my husband. He did provide all that I needed through those very difficult days but He also wanted to teach me more. It was His heart's desire that I would become betrothed to Him. This did not come easily for me nor did it come quickly. The pain of losing my husband was my primary and overwhelming

concern and I trained myself to live only one day at a time. I resisted looking into the future. God was patient with me and in His good timing I did totally yield myself to Him. It was His heart's desire to take my pain and sorrow of losing Bill, and fill the vacancy in my heart with Himself as my betrothed.

Once I had finished that book it was my heart's desire that it would be published; however, it sat on the shelf for a good long time. I used to remind Him about the book on the shelf, but He made it clear to me that He was not really eager to jump to my schedule. What He was looking for was an attitude of obedience, submission, and a willingness to wait on Him.

He finally arranged a simply divine meeting in His own sweet and perfect time. He introduced me to a publisher and she was interested in my book. How awesome is our God and His wonders will never cease!

As we were getting ready to go to print I felt the Spirit of the Lord rise up within me. It was one of those moments that cause you to bow before Him, and respond. "Yes Lord," I said, "What is it?" His response broke my heart. He said, "Some in the body of My Son are not interested in becoming betrothed to Him. They are content with where they are in their walk and are not the least bit interested in moving forward."

Have you ever felt a pang of sorrow for the Lord? Has sadness ever welled up inside of you on His behalf? Have you ever thought of how difficult it must be for Him to listen to His children constantly complaining, but seldom hearing His beloved children praising, accepting deception instead of His wonderful gifts, and arguing instead of agreeing with His wonderful plan for their lives?

Time and again reading the early scriptures will reveal that Israel, as His bride, complained bitterly, was disobedient, and downright hard to get along with. She was also stiff-necked, rebellious, and at times totally disagreeable. All in all it could not be called a happy and blissful marriage. God in His patience waited on her, but she would not move with ease into His arms. In fact Israel finally came to the place where they did not want God as husband or spiritual leader at all. They did not like being separated unto Him. They looked upon other men, other nations, and they wanted to be more like them.

The history of Israel is filled with their desire to be free of God. Israel fought with God because they wanted a change; they wanted to walk in a different direction and have more control over their own lives. Over the years God had allowed them to live under priests, prophets, and judges, but finally they asked for a king. One of the saddest conversations in the Bible took place between God and the Prophet Samuel. It begins in 1 Samuel 8, verses 6-7. *"Because the thing displeased Samuel, when they said, give us a king to judge us. And Samuel prayed unto the Lord. And the Lord said unto Samuel, hearken unto the voice of the people in all that they say unto thee, for they have not rejected thee, but they have rejected me, that I should not reign over them."*

All that God the Father had done for them was dismissed and abandoned. His power, wisdom and strength were of no interest to them anymore. They wanted different leadership and that broke His heart. If we have ever thought that God does not understand our pain then it is possible that we have never fully understood His.

In our study for this book we searched for truth about our remaining life here on earth and our future life that we will enjoy in heaven.

When the Lord Jesus descends with a trumpet blast and a shout and we are caught away, where are we going and what will we be doing there? As we know from the Bible we will be joining Jesus and His Father at the marriage supper of the Lamb, but have we prepared ourselves to be the Bride of Christ or will we be ushered out of His presence because we are not properly attired or prepared? We are not talking about a walk in the park here; we need to dig deeply, to research fully in order to understand all that God has said to us about betrothal, engagement, and marriage, so that we may show ourselves approved and gain full entry when we arrive to meet our Husband/Groom.

God the Father's greatest desire is for us to allow Jesus to take His full place as our husband. Jesus wants to love us, protect us, and to take us as wife. He wants to give us His life in exchange for our own. This He has done for me, and many others, but He also wants to do it for all His children. Somehow it seems easier for those of us who were once totally broken to fully yield to Jesus than it is for those who have never known the true heartache of great personal loss.

Hear me church, God's heart hungers for each of us to become the bride of His Son; and Jesus wants to have us as His wife. This world and even some in the church will not understand, but He does. If we will release ourselves to Him then He will lead us to relinquish all that we have in order to become the Bride of Christ.

Now is the time for all of us to prepare for the great marriage to the Lord, so that we will be able to join the Heavenly family at the soon coming Marriage Supper of the Lamb.

If there is one thing that we do not want to do it is to behave as the invitees to a wedding that Jesus spoke about in Matthew 22:2-14. Recalling the story, it was about the Kingdom of Heaven being likened unto a King who was preparing a marriage for his son. He sent out his servants to call the honored guests but they would not come. He then sent out other servants to call the guests, reminding them that all was in readiness for the guests to make their appearance. They still would not come and some even killed the servants of the King. The King was very angry so he sent his army to destroy those who had treated his servants in such a manner. Then the King explained to his servants that those who had been called obviously were not worthy. So he sent them out again to fetch all who would come, good or bad, so the wedding would be attended by guests. When all was in readiness then the King appeared in the wedding chamber to see those who had come. He immediately spotted a man who was not in wedding attire, one who had not prepared himself for such a glorious day. The King approached the man and inquired about his manner of dress and the man was speechless but the Lord was not. He called his servants to bind the man and take him away, to cast him into outer darkness where there would be weeping and gnashing of teeth. Jesus then said, *"For many are called, but few are chosen" (Matthew 22:14).*

Jesus most often spoke in parables and it is pretty obvious that in this story He is describing His Father and His Father's Kingdom. The subject is a marriage for the Son whom we know is Jesus. The descriptions of the servants that have been sent are very evidently the many evangelists, prophets, and teachers that God has sent into this world to tell the perfect story of Jesus and His love for us. I had been taught that the poor soul who was not in proper attire was lacking evidence of the Baptism of the Holy Spirit, with speaking in other tongues. However, after studying God's thoughts on weddings, I have concluded that it is as it says; he was not properly attired in wedding clothes. He was not prepared to join in the wedding of the Son. He had not readied the outer man or the inner man. It was not just his outer clothing that mattered; he had not prepared his heart to allow the Son to become his betrothed. If it had been just his rough clothing that offended the King, then he just would have been escorted out of the house. But take note that he was bound hand and foot and cast into outer darkness where there was weeping and gnashing of teeth. (See Matthew 8:12). That sounds like hell to me. If this situation mattered so much to the King then it must be very important for us to be prepared and dressed in our best wedding attire for both the inner man and outer man. I would suggest that each of us take a moment right now and ask the Lord if He wants us betrothed to Him. I pray that this book gives guidance and directions by the Holy Spirit so that each person will become yielded and prepared enough to thus become betrothed to the beloved Son of the living God before it is too late.

The Sins of Our Fathers

Before we go any further, I want to make it very clear that some of the worst mistakes made by the early Christian Church fathers were in turning our foundational studies away from the traditions of the Jews. We Christians have missed so much by not understanding every deep meaning and nuance that was hidden away in the Old Covenant and which should have been carried over as foundational into the New. We have misunderstood much of what we read because we were seldom given the proper background. Unfortunately we also held to what we knew, which was not always correct, and we had little patience with learning something new. It is really a shame because it would have helped us a great deal to understand more easily all that God wants to show us. In this book I will try to bring in as much of the Old Testament and Jewish truths as I can find that concern the issues of betrothals, marriages and their relationships to the Holy Family.

God gave all truth for a purpose and without it we really miss the actual point of each and every parable and story. When we read the New Covenant without the background of the Old then it is as if we have built a building without a solid and proper foundation. In other words, we have eaten the dessert of the New Testament without eating the full, satisfying, and life-giving meal of the Old. We will have a partial blessing but not all the greatest and best understanding that is available for us. We should also understand that the Bible was written as an eastern book, with eastern truths to submit and we with western minds

and life experiences sometimes miss the point. It needs to be noted that the Bible was written to three people - the Jew, the Nations also called the Gentiles and the Church. It is imperative that we truly understand the differences between that which was written for each of the groups.

In the year 306 A.D. Constantine became Emperor of Rome. He was called a man of valor, a strong warrior and was highly esteemed by the men who fought under him. It has been written that on the night before an important battle Constantine had a dream in which he was commanded to put the sign of Christ's cross on his soldiers' shields. It has also been written that while his army was marching to the battlefield they saw a sign in the sky. It was a light cross with the words, *By this sign you will be victor.* Whichever story is true, he did as he was told and he won this battle so decisively that he became the ruling monarch of the entire known world at that time. Constantine gave all of the credit to *the God of the Christians.* It was then that he declared himself to be a Christian. He called for the end of all Roman persecution against the Christians which had been not just tolerated, but enjoyed by the Romans for too many years. Glory be to God! We have all heard and read about the dreadful atrocities that were wrought against Christians in those days. It made the Roman population happy and kept them from causing trouble against the local authorities. The killing and mutilation of Christians was called for by the Caesars, under the guise of sport. But in truth, it was a method for ethnic cleansing. Previous emperors had enjoyed watching the killing of Christians and the crowds always cheered the loudest while watching the meek and powerless being crushed, mutilated and killed by the most powerful.

Constantine also declared that Rome and all her territories would be called Christian. His mother had become a Christian before him and her faith was very strong. He accepted Christ basically because of the signs and wonders that had led him into victory and also because his mother had faithfully prayed that he should follow her in kind. Though Constantine declared his faith, it is interesting to note that he delayed his baptism which apparently was not uncommon in that day. Some say he used that ploy because he well knew that as Emperor he would do much that could be considered unacceptable or unrighteous; so he delayed his baptism until near the end of his life. It is also interesting to note that though he professed a faith in Christ, he continued to worship and pay homage to the pagan gods of Rome. He worshiped Mars and Apollo, who were major deities in the Roman area of influence.

But by declaring the Roman state to be a Christian state, Constantine unknowingly created enormous confusion between Christians and pagans. On the one hand many of the Roman Christians were overwhelmed with the events of the day. They were convinced that since this great victory had happened so quickly and since Constantine had given their God all the glory, then the Lord Jesus would be returning very quickly. They believed that since the Kingdom of God was then in control of the whole known world, He would come at any moment. They had accepted the following scripture as having been fulfilled: *"The kingdoms of this world are become the kingdoms of our Lord, and of his Christ; and he shall reign for ever and ever."* (Revelation 11:15b). This shows us how easily we can miss it in the reading of the Holy Scriptures.

On the other hand, people who were not really born again believers, but were indeed lovers of pagan gods, were then being lumped together and called Christian. In order to appease one or the other of the religious groups Constantine had ordered that the days of Christian celebrations would fall upon the days of the religious holidays that the pagans were accustomed to using. This made the final break between the early Christian church and her Jewish roots. Unfortunately it has taken many years to begin the trip back into wholeness,

Jew and Gentile, all children of Abraham under the mantle of God, our King.

The overall history of the church is ripe with gross atrocities against the Jewish people. For example, during the days of the Crusaders, the Soldiers of the Cross could not distinguish between Jew and Arab. Though it was the Muslims they were after, they killed equally as many Jews. Also in Spain during a time called the Inquisition, the Church was so politically powerful they were able to kill the Jews and steal all their possessions unless they would accept their Christian view. Even in our own time many of the top ranking members of Hitler's staff were so-called church members. The Jewish people suffered enormously under their hands. This is really not the place to write in detail about these things; however, it would be wise to study our own history to better understand why the Jewish people had such great fear of things known to be Christian.

But we of course must never lose sight of the fact that Jesus laid down His own life for us. Though we were yet sinners, He died for us and no man took His life from Him! *"As the Father knoweth me, even so know I the Father: and I lay down my life for the sheep. And other sheep I have, which are not of this fold: them also I must bring, and they shall hear my voice; and there shall be one fold, and one shepherd. Therefore doth my Father love me, because I lay down my life, that I might take it again. No man taketh it from me, but I lay it down of myself. I have power to lay it down, and I have power to take it again. This commandment have I received of my Father"* (John 10:15-18).

In this book we will learn about the original feasts and celebrations and will find how they fall according to God's calendar. All of the Hebrew holy days, festive celebrations and commemorations fall in springtime and then again in autumn. These celebrations were given to the Hebrew children while they were still in an arid desert, which was unsuitable for any kind of farming. Nevertheless, God called for His great celebrations to fall on a yearly cycle of seed planting and harvesting. The change in those dates was slight, but the error was great.

Let me explain. We all know that the New Covenant scripture tells us that Jesus was the Passover lamb according to 1 Corinthians 5:7. But since we do not study about the Passover, which is in the Old Covenant or Old Testament written in Exodus 12, then what does that mean to those of us who have not been taught to understand?

For example, one of our most highly valued Christian rites is called the Holy Communion, the Eucharist, or the Lord's Supper. What is the background of this most holy communion with God and where did it come from? Most Christians do not know that the taking of bread and wine as the Body of Christ came from the Passover Seder. When Jesus took the bread, which was called the *bread of affliction,* it was from the Afikomen. When He took the cup it was the third cup from the Seder meal called the *cup of redemption.* Now when we partake of the bread and wine we are able to fully appreciate the treasured meanings of the Lord's Holy Communion.

We can learn more about the Seder meal by accepting invitations to attend. Those of us who may know Messianic Jews, or have friends within the traditional Jewish community, could express interest and try to get invited to their family Seder. I will write more about this later.

Also we Christians celebrate the resurrection of Christ on a day that was reserved for worship of a pagan goddess. She was Ishtar who was worshiped in the springtime because she was the goddess of fertility. That is why we celebrate with eggs, a well-known sign of fertility; and the rabbit, of course, is one of the most fertile creatures on the planet. We do not celebrate the resurrection of Jesus on the day He arose, which was the

Day of Early First Fruits. That is a Jewish Celebration created by God and written about in Leviticus 23:16-21. Early First Fruits was perfectly fulfilled when Jesus rose from the dead on that day and He was called by Paul the First Fruit from God in 1 Corinthians 15:20-23. Do we celebrate on that day? No, we do not! We celebrate the remarkable resurrection of Jesus on the pagan holiday for the goddess of fertility.

We can also look at Pentecost, a special day that the Jews call Shavuot. This is an old and great Jewish anniversary that recalls the day when God created the world; and on that anniversary God gave them the great gift of the Law while they were at Mt. Sinai. The correct day of Pentecost is calculated by counting fifty days from the second day of Passover. This is called the counting of the Omer. The counting of the fifty days is to begin with the Passover season; however, we Christians begin the count at Easter, which means that we are generally off by a few days. Does it matter? I think so but this is not the place to elaborate in detail. A little study will reveal that our worship is a little askew and has been for centuries.

These facts are well known by the leaders of our faith, so I ask that everyone reading this book not to go to pastors and tell them the Christian calendar is not accurate. Every pastor is probably well aware of this situation and can do nothing about it because these traditions have been set as if in concrete for so long that it would be almost impossible to change them now. In truth it would be like opening a can of worms. No matter the day, we need to study all of the Jewish feasts, commemorative days and holy convocations because these are the times that we will celebrate in Heaven. We need to be accustomed to them. We must also understand what they mean. My prayer is that no one will be fooled or deceived about this truth. When we do get to Heaven we will not keep the traditions of men; we will instead surely keep these wonderful godly feasts.

Let me give one more example of the error in the Christian calendar. Most of us can recall God named only one day of the week. He named the last day of the week the Shabbat which means to cease or desist, in other words, to enter God's rest. All the other days he numbered as we read in Genesis 2:2-3. The Jews were to worship and rest on Shabbat. We have named our day of worship the Sabbath, thinking that it is as the Shabbat that God called for, a day of worship and rest. This is incorrect. We actually worship on the first day of the week called Sunday because that was the day that pagan Rome worshiped the Sun god and that is where that day gets its name. We rise on Sunday to go to worship as if it were Shabbat. Originally many thought that the Christians chose that day because it was on a Sunday that Jesus rose from the dead, but in truth we were given a pagan day in order to rise up and worship our wonderful God.

The mistakes made against Israel by the early church are not the only mistakes made against the Jews by the church. Some dreadful mistakes are being made right now. There are those who believe in the so-called Replacement theology, which says that the church has replaced Israel in the heart of God. Those who believe this way are absolutely wrong. Israel will always be in the very center of God's heart and there will come a day when the whole world will know it. *"And it shall come to pass in that day, that I will seek to destroy all the nations that come against Jerusalem. And I will pour upon the house of David, and upon the inhabitants of Jerusalem, the spirit of grace and of supplications: and they shall look upon me whom they have pierced, and they shall mourn for him, as one mourneth for his only son, and shall be in bitterness for him, as one that is in bitterness for his firstborn. In that day shall there be a great mourning in Jerusalem, as the mourning of Hadadrimmon in the valley of Megiddon"* (Zechariah 12:9-11).

And if that is not enough for us then hear this, *"And from Jesus Christ, who is the faithful witness, and the first begotten of the dead, and the prince of the kings of the earth. Unto him that loved us, and washed us from our sins in his own blood, And hath made us kings and priests unto God and his Father; to him be glory and dominion for ever and ever. Amen. Behold, he cometh with clouds; and every eye shall see him, and they also which pierced him: and all kindreds of the earth shall wail because of him. Even so, Amen"* (Revelation 1:5-7). This shows agreement with both the Old and New Testaments concerning God's unfailing love toward his chosen people and the nation of Israel. God was a faithful bridegroom and he was a faithful husband, though in many ways Israel turned away from Him, however, God remains steadfast in His love for her.

One of the most difficult challenges for those of us who love Israel is to watch some Christians support the enemies of Israel under the mistaken belief that they, the church, have replaced Israel in God's heart. Because of this they choose to support Arab and Muslim nations who want nothing more than to push the Jews into the sea. A most earnest time of prayer is ahead for the true church and for the nation of Israel. If people are seekers of truth or confused about the history of Israel and are weary of hearing constant repetition of mistaken accounts made by the enemies of Israel let us be clear; the best true book about Israel, aside from the Bible, is a book called *The Source*, written by James A. Michener.

Michener's book is a true account of the history of Israel from the times of the cavemen until just after the creation of Israel as a state. Michener tells the story about those last days before statehood as the Jews begged the Arabs who were soon to become refugees, not to take that fateful step but to stay and rebuild a nation with them. Even today there are Arabs serving in the Knesset of Israel which is the highest governing body of the land. And when people walk down any street they will find shops side by side, which are owned by Muslim, Christian and Jew. The Arab people who stayed have been blessed. However, those who left, those who have taken on the name of Palestinians for example, are still seeking a homeland.

In obedience to the leaders of their mosques they ran away because their highest religious authority had told them to leave. They were told that once they left they would join with Syria and the other Arab nations who would unite to make war against the Jews. They would overwhelm them and drive the Jews into the sea. This has been tried again and again, but God's beloved Israel still stands as the lone democracy in the area. Israel stands almost alone and her enemies grow as the years go by. Please pray for Israel as the Lord Himself has ordered, *"Pray for the peace of Jerusalem: they shall prosper that love thee" (Psalm 122:6).*

In our Bibles we can find a map of Jerusalem. Notice the strange looking darkened area made up of the Hinnon, the Tyropoeon, and the Kidron Valleys. Then look to Psalm 119:161 and note the Hebrew letter Shin, which is shaped as an artistic "w". Now compare it to the darkened area in the map of Jerusalem. I once sat on a large rock of marble in that area. The leader told me that I was sitting on the name of God.

I quickly stood to my feet as my guide, George Horesh, showed me in my own Bible the remarkable signature of God, which God Himself had marked in the city of Jerusalem. We can see how the valleys resemble the Shin. This letter is pronounced "Sheen" and it is the first letter in the word Shaddai. When a Jew calls upon the name of his Lord, he calls for El Shaddai, "God Almighty".

We have heard it said that God wrote His name in Israel; Jerusalem is where He did it. He wrote the first letter of His name in the heart of Jerusalem using her hills and valleys. It's as if He scratched His initial in the city that He loves. Proof is in the land that it is God's and should not be divided among others. For further study, quotes can be found in 1 Kings 11:36, 2 Kings 21:4, 2 Chronicles 6:6, and 2 Chronicles 33:4.

Someday this will all be made right and God Himself will correct it. There will be a great day on which we will be called away from this fouled earth to join Him in Heaven for the greatest moment yet to come, the Marriage Supper of the Lamb. I pray that we are obedient to His call but before the great trumpet sounds we should be as the wise virgins in Matthew 25:1-13. Our lamps need to be full of oil and we would be wise to have extra oil in our vessels so when Jesus comes to collect His Bride we will not be found sleeping. Let us be prepared and ready to celebrate at the marriage supper as the wife of our beloved faithful Lord, for He is worthy.

Many people probably wonder why God chose Israel as the favorite and promised land. It was basically because geographically that area was the only true land bridge between Africa and Asia and then on to Europe. When God created the earth He made for Himself an area that would be the very center of the old world and that is why Israel is often called the navel of the earth. It was the very best location from which He could send out the news that the Jews were the chosen people and that God had selected them to send out the great truth that the future Jewish Messiah was destined to become the Saviour of the world.

The Sins of our Fathers

Ancient Jewish Weddings

*I*n order to better understand the true meaning of betrothal and marriage, one must study ancient Hebrew weddings. After all, God Himself gave the instructions for all segments of Jewish life. There were commandments, laws and ordinances. These would be strictly obeyed through birth, dedication and/or circumcision, and bar or bat mitzvah, through to adult lives or when death intervened. Some sages wrote that early Israeli marriages really satisfied their law more than they did their religion. However, the rabbis did consider weddings in Israel as sacred and taught that God watched over every wedding and His blessings were upon the groom and his bride.

I would like to point out that women in those days had very little say about their own lives. It has been reported that the first thing a Jewish man often said in the morning as he arose from his bed was, *Thank God I am not a dog or a woman.* That pretty much tells of the general thinking about women in that day. Their opinions were seldom sought and their word had little value in a court of law.

Let us look at a very early picture of the male/female relationship. It is about the visit of two angels to the house of Lot when he lived in Sodom. *"But before they lay down, the men of the city, even the men of Sodom, compassed the house round, both old and young, all the people from every quarter: And they called unto Lot, and said unto him, Where are the men which came in to thee this night? bring them out unto us, that we may know them. And Lot went out at the door unto them, and shut the door*

after him, And said, I pray you, brethren, do not so wickedly. Behold now, I have two daughters which have not known man; let me, I pray you, bring them out unto you, and do ye to them as is good in your eyes: only unto these men do nothing; for therefore came they under the shadow of my roof. And they said, Stand back. And they said again, This one fellow came in to sojourn, and he will needs be a judge: now will we deal worse with thee, than with them. And they pressed sore upon the man, even Lot, and came near to break the door. But the men put forth their hand, and pulled Lot into the house to them, and shut to the door" (Genesis 19:4-10). It could be that Lot freely offered his daughters because he knew that the Sodomites would have no interest in them. That may be true in part. However as I understand it, the Middle East societal traditions in those days called for a strict adherence to their code of hospitality. The protection of one's guests was supreme even over the lives of the female members of a household. Even today, as we watch the news we can see that not much has changed in that area of the world. The rules of hospitality are still very strong and we can still see that women have very little control over their own lives.

Now as we look at the areas of betrothal and marriage in the Jewish tradition we find that it was usually the father of the groom who selected the bride. For reasons of love, wealth or social standing, he would be the one to make the selection of his son's bride. Jamie Lash in her book entitled, *The Ancient Jewish Wedding... and the Return of Messiah for His Bride*, noted that as Jesus said, *"Ye have not chosen me, but I have chosen you, and ordained you, that ye should go and bring forth fruit, and that your fruit should remain: that whatsoever ye shall ask of the Father in my name, he may give it you." (John 15:16).*

Often in the early days the bride and groom did not even know each other and they likely would not have seen each other until the waited-for moment, the moment of the betrothal. In a situation such as this the only contact that the bride had with her would-be groom was through the servant or friend of the groom who had been sent to fetch her. It was through expressions of respect, love and loyalty from the mouth of the groomsman that the bride would learn about the goodness of her beloved. The story written in Genesis 24 tells us how Rebekah first heard about Isaac. And in truth, we must not overlook the fact that this is exactly how we met Jesus; we first heard about Him whom we had not seen, then we believed on Him, and finally we accepted Him into our hearts, *"Whom having not seen, ye love; in whom, though now ye see him not, yet believing, ye rejoice with joy unspeakable and full of glory:"* (1 Peter 1:8).

Following Jewish tradition the groom and bride, once the price was paid and the cup was shared, became betrothed. Then the groom could go to build a suitable home for his bride. Often the home was a room attached to the groom's family home, and when the groom had completed the work to his father's satisfaction, then the groom would go and get his betrothed bride in order to proceed with the wedding.

Some marriages were forbidden by law. An example is a marriage between relatives who were too close in family relationship, as found in Leviticus 20:14. Deuteronomy 25:6 tells us that some marriages were obligated by law; for instance, if a man died without leaving an heir, his brother was expected to marry the widow to raise up posterity of the deceased. Here again it appears that women really did not have much to say about the direction of their lives but the following stories will show that there were some who were well able to stand against even the wiliest of men.

In his book, *Daily Life in the Time of Jesus*, Henri Daniel-Rops wrote three interesting stories. The first one gives a real definition of rabbinical thinking concerning women. As the story goes, "The Lord gave ten measures of words for the whole of humanity; the women seized upon nine of them. Greedy and idle, jealous and quarrelsome, that describes women: they also listen behind doors." The second story is as follows; "From which part of the man shall I take the woman?" the Almighty asked Himself. "From the head? She would be too proud. From the eye? She would be too inquisitive. From the ear? She would eavesdrop. From the mouth? She would be garrulous. From the hand? She would be wasteful." In the end He took a very obscure, well-hidden part of the body, in hopes of making her modest.

This is one of my favorite stories, in defense of women, and it came as a charming fable attributed to Gamaliel, the master of the apostle Paul. An emperor said to a wise man, "Thy God is a thief; to make a woman he had to steal a rib from the sleeping Adam."

The doctor did not know what to answer, but his daughter said, "Let me take care of this." She went to see the emperor and said to him, "We call for justice."

"Indeed? What for?" asked the emperor.

"Thieves got into our house in the night. They have taken away a silver ewer and they have left a gold one in its place."

"Ha, ha," said the emperor, "I wish I could have burglars like that every night."

"Well," said the girl, "That is what our God did. He took a mere rib from the first man, but in exchange he gave him a wife."

It was mandatory that before any wedding could properly take place, there would be a frank discussion of the bridal price. Some think that this was a gift made to the father of the bride. However, it was truly a purchase price since in those days women were considered as possessions, as again reiterated in Jamie Lash's book. She also pointed out that in the Tenth Commandment, God mentioned wives in the list of possessions that were not to be lusted over. *"Thou shalt not covet thy neighbour's house, thou shalt not covet thy neighbour's wife, nor his manservant, nor his maidservant, nor his ox, nor his ass, nor any thing that is thy neighbour's" (Exodus 20:17).*

She also revealed that the Hebrew word for wife is translated as the "owned one" and husband is translated as "master" or "owner". Jamie continues by saying, this might seem cruel in today's culture, but it was actually a step above what was happening in the pagan world where a man could just take whom he wanted, have intercourse with her and if he chose to keep her then she was considered his wife until his eyes fell upon another.

Knowing the proper translation of husband as owner makes it a lot clearer and easier to understand why Sarah spoke of Abraham as Lord. (See Genesis 18:12). He had very likely paid a goodly sum for her and she was responding as a wife who understood that her husband indeed owned her. I have heard it taught that Sarah was referring to Abraham as if he were a precursor to Jesus because of his strong relationship with God. If the teacher had understood the true Hebrew translation that the husband was her owner then the teaching could have borne more fruit.

We must never forget that we who have become born again are in many ways like a Jewish bride. Our intended groom has already paid a great price for us and in the paying Jesus gave us His life. I found it fascinating that again in that wonderful little book by Jamie Lash concerning ancient Jewish weddings she wrote about the last words that Jesus spoke on the cross. She said that Jesus paid a mohar (mow-haar), a price for us, His Bride, on the cross. In saying, *It is finished!* the word that He spoke came from the root word, ka'lal which means to complete, make perfect or finish. It is the same root of the word for bride, kallah. She asks, could Yeshua's last word on the cross have had bridal overtones? Was His bride, the church, His last thought as He paid the bride price for her? How awesome it is to know that Jesus went through all of that with us on His mind. *We give our thanks and praise to You Almighty Lord that the price for the bride of Christ is already paid!*

In the early days some thought that the relationship of bride and groom was like the relationship between Jehovah and his people. The early rabbinic writers so often wrote about this that the bridal couple usually thought of themselves as representing God and Israel. I have heard it said that God Himself had spoken the words of blessing over the cup at the union of our first parents, when Michael and Gabriel acted as groomsmen, and the angelic choir sang the wedding hymn.

The pious that prepared to be wed were faithful to confess their sins and keep to their fast before the wedding. The bride and groom had been kept apart, sometimes even for the full year allowed by law; the bride would keep busy in preparation for the wedding day and the groom in building their future home.

The Jews were also taught that to marry was as a personal Yom Kippur (Yome Kee-poor), since entrance into the marriage state was thought to carry the forgiveness of sin. Yom Kippur is the holiest day of the year and is the only time during which Jews can receive full atonement for their sins. How grateful they will be when they finally meet Jesus. Praise You Lord!

Also when a bride and groom and their wedding procession passed by, then by Israelite law all those who saw them would quickly stand and clap their hands. Even if they were in a company of mourners, they would stop, turn to the happy couple, and clap their hands. Marriage and weddings carried the full blessing of God and obedience to the law was required.

When we read 2 Kings 9:35, we will see that the only body parts which remained after the death of Queen Jezebel were her head, her hands and her feet. Though her sins were like crimson before the Lord it is thought that these body parts remained simply because she honored the law when she stood and clapped her hands in joy as a wedding party passed by. Marriage was considered the highest act performed by a young couple. They would be faithfully following the admonition of God to marry and populate the world.

The Jewish wedding had two distinctly separate parts; the betrothal came first and the marriage followed. At the betrothal the bridegroom, or his agent, would hand the bride a letter declaring his love, and a small gift and/or a piece of money. These items would express the intent of the bridegroom to marry this young woman. Once the bridegroom had made his intentions clear then he could present to the father of the bride, the ketubah (ke-tube-ah), which was a legal and binding contract. This document would be presented to the father of the bride for his perusal and agreement. In it the groom pledged that he would work for his bride, honor her, keep her, and care for her as in the manner of the men of Israel. He would promise to give her a sum of money and the groom would then guarantee that if she were poor, he would increase her dowry by at least one half, using all of his own possessions to serve as guarantee. When the father and the bride agreed with the contract and signed it, this Ketubah would adorn the walls of the bride's new home. These were beautifully decorated printed documents and if there were ever a disagreement the bride would check the promises of the ketubah.

Once the father of the intended bride was satisfied, he would fill a cup with wine and wait to see if the proposal was accepted. The intended groom would drink from the cup; if the young woman decided in favor, then the intended bride also drank. Under the terms of Jewish law they were now espoused or betrothed. Some say this could be called an engagement, however the rules were far more stringent and more legally binding than any form of engagement that I know of. From this moment on the bride and groom were treated as if they were indeed married except in the area of sexual intimacy. This is considered to be the manner in which Joseph proposed and then was accepted by Mary. If the answer was yes, as it was between Joseph and Mary and once they sipped from the cup, they were betrothed.

It is interesting to note that God protects all males who are betrothed and readying for marriage:

"When thou goest out to battle against thine enemies, and seest horses, and chariots, and a people more than thou, be not afraid of them: for the LORD thy God is with thee, which brought thee up out of the land of Egypt. And it shall be, when ye are come nigh unto the battle, that the priest shall approach and speak unto the people, And shall say unto them, Hear, O Israel, ye approach this day unto battle against your enemies: let not your hearts faint, fear not, and do not tremble, neither be ye terrified because of them; For the LORD your God is he that goeth with you, to fight for you against your enemies, to save you. And the officers shall speak unto the people, saying, What man is there that hath built a new house, and hath not dedicated it? let him go and return to his house, lest he die in the battle, and another man dedicate it. And what man is he that hath planted a vineyard, and hath not yet eaten of it? let him also go and return unto his house, lest he die in the battle, and another man eat of it. And what man is there that hath betrothed a wife, and hath not taken her? let him go and return unto his house, lest he die in the battle, and

another man take her (Deuteronomy 20:1-7). These words were of great comfort to both the bride and the groom.

After betrothal the groom leaves the bride until their wedding day. She would only hear of him through reports from their friends. She and her family would prepare and wait for the great day when she would be called to the wedding. The bride would be taught about how to be a good and caring wife. Secrets would be shared between mother and daughter and if she did not already know how to sew and cook, then she would learn. During this time of her preparation the bride and her family would stay very close as she longed for the special time ahead.

At this same time the groom would be working hard preparing a proper home for them both. It is interesting to note that it is not the groom who makes the decision about the readiness of the new home; it is his father who makes that decision. Many say that the groom would likely slap together a few boards and call it suitable; but the father of the groom wants his son to prepare a proper place in order for God to bless the union of the groom and his bride. Some readers may notice that this story is very reminiscent of the remarks of Jesus when He left this earth. Jesus said, *"In my Father's house are many mansions: if it were not so, I would have told you. I go to prepare a place for you. And if I go and prepare a place for you, I will come again, and receive you unto myself; that where I am, there ye may be also"* (John 14:2-3).

Joy everlasting, Jesus is even now preparing a place for us. He works to create a proper place so that when we make that final great pilgrimage to Heaven a fine and proper home awaits us. Some say it will be a mansion and others say it will be just a room, but whatever it will be it will perfectly fit our needs. We too must wait just as the Jewish bride must wait for her intended. And as the Jewish bride we must work to become prepared to be the Bride of Christ. When that great trumpet sounds and we hear the final shout that the "Bridegroom cometh," we will be ready. *"For the Lord Himself shall descend from heaven with a shout, and the voice of the archangel, and with the trump of God: and the dead in Christ shall rise first: Then we which are alive and remain shall be caught up together with them in the clouds, to meet the Lord in the air: and so shall we ever be with the Lord. Wherefore comfort one another with these words"* (1 Thessalonians 4:16-18).

When a Jewish bride first sensed that her wedding time was near she began her final preparations. She washed herself in the family mikvah (mick-vah). The mikvah was a bath that was used for ritual cleansing. Each home was to have one; their style and size would depend upon financial circumstances. Some were elegant and ornate while others would be plain but serviceable. Both bride and groom would visit a mikvah in preparation for their marriage so that they could come together not only physically, but ritually clean.

At the proper time for the actual marriage, usually at night, the groom or his appointed groomsman would be preceded by the sound of the trumpet which could be heard when they arrived at the home of the bride. He would then lead her from her paternal home to the home of her would-be husband. As they walk along together there would be sounds of music and the bride would be modestly covered with the bridal veil. Her hair would be long and flowing, and she would walk in the midst of her friends.

Soon those in the wedding party would be united with the *friends of the bridegroom* and they would walk as a happy and festive crowd. Some would hold torches and there could be lamps on poles, while the bride and groom would be festooned with flowers. Those nearest to them would be carrying festive myrtle branches. When it would go unnoticed the groom would secretly lift a corner of her veil and take a quick peek just to be absolutely certain that he had the right woman. We all remember the story in Genesis 29:21-25 when Jacob, who thought he was marrying Rachel, ended up with Leah as his first wife. No well-intentioned young Jewish groom wants to follow that tradition. All who saw them pass would arise and join in the festivities; they would salute the bride and recognize her beauty, as was their religious duty.

Upon entering the groom's home the bride would quickly survey the room to see family and childhood friends. She would happily notice the bridal room, which was to become her special room. It was probably the room that had been painstakingly built by her groom, and now it was beautifully decorated with candles, food and flowers. It was built to be their first home, but it was set up and prepared for their first week together. In the early years there would be no Chuppa (Hoopa) under which they would stand to be wed. There would be a gift to the groom, a new white Tallit (Tall-eet) which was carefully made by his bride. This Tallit would be lifted up over their heads as they shared the final wedding cup and then it would become his personal prayer shawl through all his days as her husband.

At this time, the groom would give her a gift of gold, possibly a plain undecorated simple ring which he would place on the forefinger of her right hand. He would then accept her according to the Law of Moses and Israel. A proclamation affirming this would be spoken. The bride and groom would be crowned with garlands, as if they were king and queen.

If the ketubah (ke-tube-ah) had not been given at the time of the betrothal, then before the wedding could proceed this legal document would be affirmed and signed by the groom and witnessed by at least two men. The ketubah is also reminiscent of the scripture used by Moses as a covenant between God and the Jewish people.

We, the Bride of Christ, have a wonderful gift from our groom; it is the beloved Holy Spirit. And our ketubah is the New Covenant in which God promises to love us, care for us, meet all of our needs and watch over us daily. The Bride of Christ has all the guarantees that her Jewish sisters have, but ours is as a covenant signed in blood. His Blood!

After the prescribed washing of the hands then the young couple stood side by side under the new white Tallit for the first time. The groom entered first and the bride followed into the wedding area where she stood on his right side. A cup would be filled and a solemn prayer called the Bridal Benediction would be spoken over it. And once the couple had sipped from the cup then the wedding would be over. Since the earliest of times to signal the end of the ceremony, bridegrooms have broken a glass with their foot. These were wrapped in white linen in order to contain the fragments of the broken glass. It is thought that the cup that was to be broken was the cup that they used for their earlier betrothal ceremony. Some say that this act demonstrated that the newly married couple stood no longer as single individuals with walls separating them, but in marriage, all of the walls having been broken down and standing as one. Others think it is a symbolic act reminding all those present of the sad destruction of the Temple. It is interesting to note that today some even use a light bulb because it makes a clearer sound.

Once the marriage is completed then the happy couple would be overwhelmed with shouts of "Mazel Tov (Maltzelle Tove)," which brings the blessing of good luck. After everyone had a moment with the newlywed couple, the friend of the groom would then escort the bride and groom to their bridal chamber. When they entered they would be left alone together for seven full days, a time called the *Week of the Bride*. The friend of the bridegroom would close the door then wait at the door of the wedding chamber to hear the groom announce that the marriage had been consummated. And in unison the guests would happily shout, "Mazel Tov" and then they would leave them in God's hands to learn about each other and begin their new lives together.

When the week together was over and the newlyweds were ready for company then it was time for the marriage supper. Everything would be ready for the joy of the feast. There would be music, food, wine, dancing and great celebration and joy. The marriage supper was measured by the wealth of the family and sometimes the feast lasted well over a day. Each guest offered a contribution for the enjoyment of the occasion. Some say the offerings were in food and others say it was money.

This seems to be the basic plan for a wedding in the days of ancient Israel. An invitation to a modern Jewish wedding would reveal many new things, but the basic ceremony has changed very little over the years.

As is noted at the beginning of this book there is a quote from Revelation 19:7-9. *"Let us be glad and rejoice, and give honour to him: for the marriage of the Lamb is come, and his wife hath made herself ready. And to her was granted that she should be arrayed in fine linen, clean and white: for the fine linen is the righteousness of saints. And he saith unto me, Write, Blessed are they which are called unto the marriage supper of the Lamb. And he saith unto me, These are the true sayings of God."*

We as the Bride of Christ will soon be called up to the Marriage Supper of the Lamb. His call will resound throughout the world but only those who know Him will hear that great trumpet call. The dead in Christ shall rise first and then those of us who are alive on the earth will be caught up with Him and taken from this cursed place to live eternally with Him. We will be escorted to meet the friends of the bridegroom. We will also meet the archangels, the great patriarchs, the early prophets, the kings, the disciples, and of course the blessed Holy Father. It seems to be beyond natural reality; however, it is the reality of God. We the Bride of Christ will indeed be caught up to be alone with Him for the prescribed seven days... some say that it's really seven years... and we will become as one.

As young Jewish girls prepared themselves for the great day, so we as the Bride of Christ must become prepared for the time ahead and that week alone with Him! *Hallelujah to the Lamb of God, who is our Lord and Who even now, readies Himself as our beloved Bridegroom!*

The question is, are we prepared?

Introduction of the Hebrew Children

By way of introduction, allow me to explain how the Hebrew children came to find themselves as slaves in Egypt. Genesis 46 is a fascinating story about a man named Jacob, who was the father of many children. God once met with Jacob in the wilderness and changed his name to Israel, and then He promised him that Israel would become a great nation.

A moment of jealousy led some of the sons of Israel into a hateful plan to kill their youngest brother Joseph, who happened to be their father's favorite. God took an interest and became involved, so instead of death, Joseph was sold to a passing caravan as a slave instead of being killed by his brothers.

This great story shows how God turned the treachery of brothers into very good fortune, both for the family of Israel, and also for all of us who have since come into the family of God, dwelling in the blessings of Abraham.

A man named Potipher bought Joseph, and gave him authority over his household. Potipher's wife took a fancy to this young Jew, and when he refused her, she lied about his intentions toward her, so Potipher had him imprisoned. Under the favor of God, he eventually managed the prison in which he was held as a captive.

Then he was brought into the court of Pharaoh. Present day Egyptologists have differing opinions on who was the reigning Pharaoh during the time of Joseph, but for our story, that face is not important.

Through the gift of interpretation Joseph became an instrument of blessing for Pharaoh. God led Joseph in a divine plan to save Egypt from seven years of severe famine. Upon hearing the plan Pharaoh placed all of Egypt into Joseph's hands, and only Pharaoh ruled above him in power. Because of that experience the Pharaohs were grateful to the memory of Joseph and for many years they respected the children of Israel.

Time passed and few Egyptians remembered Joseph. When this story begins the Hebrew people had not only lost favor with the Pharaohs of Egypt, but had become their slaves.

If inclined, follow along with a Bible and read the story of Moses, the Hebrew children, the plagues that were brought by God, and finally the departure from the land of Egypt and beyond. The entire story from which this book took root, begins in the Book of Exodus with the birth of Moses and finishing with the marriage of God to His people at Mount Sinai.

Introduction of the Hebrew Children

God Has a Plan

"*And it came to pass in process of time, that the king of Egypt died: and the children of Israel sighed by reason of the bondage, and they cried, and their cry came up unto God by reason of the bondage. And God heard their groaning, and God remembered his covenant with Abraham, with Isaac, and with Jacob. And God looked upon the children of Israel, and God had respect unto them*" (Exodus 2:23-25).

"Now Moses kept the flock of Jethro his father in law, the priest of Midian: and he led the flock to the backside of the desert, and came to the mountain of God, even at Horeb. And the angel of the LORD appeared unto him in a flame of fire out of the midst of a bush: and he looked, and, behold, the bush burned with fire, and the bush was not consumed. And Moses said, I will now turn aside, and see this great sight, why the bush is not burnt" (Exodus 3:1-3).

Jamie Buckingham once taught us that dried brush in the wilderness would often catch on fire. The sun would reflect upon the mica, which was in the surrounding sand and then it would burn the dried brush. The great difference was that the natural brush was consumed. When Moses saw this supernatural spectacle from God, the bush was burning, but was not consumed.

When God saw that Moses had stopped to look at the fire, He said to him, "Remove your shoes from your feet for this is holy ground." Then He introduced himself to Moses saying that He was the God of his father, the God of Abraham, and the God of Isaac and the God of Jacob; and Moses hid his face for he was afraid. God then said He had heard the cry of His people in Egypt

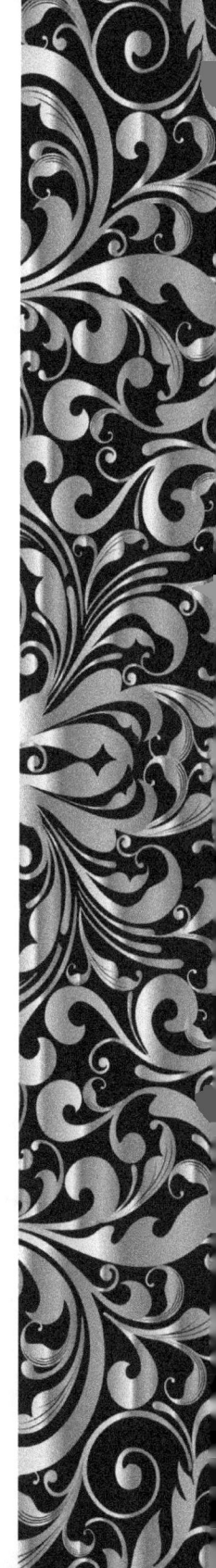

because of the burdens of the taskmasters. God told Moses that He understood their grief and their sorrow and that He wanted to deliver His people and take them out of Egypt and bring them into a good land flowing with milk and honey. He called Moses into the great work that He had for him, to go and fetch His children out of Egypt, as we read in Exodus 3:1-10.

This is the beginning of a wonderful story about God and His faithfulness. His heart's desire was to free His children from the oppression brought on by the hands of the Egyptian taskmasters. He wanted to set His people free so that they could become His bride, and He in turn would cherish and love them. He promised He would give them a land blessed with a fullness of natural resources in which they could flourish and live in peace. All they had to do was to say, *Yes, I accept.*

God chose Moses to be His groomsman, or friend of the groom, to lead the Hebrew children, His bride, out of bondage and into perpetual love and joy with Him. Many years before Moses had been born the son of slaves, and under the law of Egypt he should have been put to death. However, with God's miraculous protection the baby was given into the hands of Pharaoh's daughter. She took him and once weaned, she reared him as her own son. He grew up as the grandson of Pharaoh before all the rulers of Egypt, but he lived under the favor of God. God saw to it that this son of Levi would become His strong arm throughout the fight that he would one day have with the Pharaoh of Egypt. The plan was born in God's heart way before it was required; God saw that at the perfect time, Israel would be delivered to become His precious bride.

The question remains: Did Moses yield immediately so that God might make him the proper ambassador to Pharaoh? The answer is No. He, like all of us, felt ill-equipped to handle the job God had for him. Moses felt as if he were destined to set the Hebrew children free. He had once killed an Egyptian who was mistreating one of his Hebrew brothers, but when that act became known, he fled into the land of Midian, as recorded in Exodus 2:11-14. God called Moses to return to Egypt and lead His people out. Moses expressed uncertainty. Those (40) years in the desert had taken the zealous fire out of him and he felt as if he were unable to do what God asked. He doubted that he could convince the Hebrews that God had really sent him. Most of us would have felt the same way, but do we doubt our abilities? Or do we doubt that God will really lead us through to complete the great assignment? We often have more trust in that which we can see with our natural eyes, rather than trust in spiritual sight of God's plans.

God encouraged Moses and gave him the name in which to convince the Hebrews. *"And God said unto Moses, I AM THAT I AM: and he said, Thus shalt thou say unto the children of Israel, I AM hath sent me unto you. And God said moreover unto Moses, Thus shalt thou say unto the children of Israel, The LORD God of your fathers, the God of Abraham, the God of Isaac, and the God of Jacob, hath sent me unto you: this is my name for ever, and this is my memorial unto all generations" (Exodus 3:14-15).*

God told Moses that He would send him to bring His children out of the land of Egypt and that he should use His name, the name of God, so that the Hebrew children would accept that he truly represented God. By that name they would believe him and be willing to allow Moses to lead them out of bondage (see Exodus 3:21-22). He also told him to gather the elders of the Hebrew people together and tell them that God had not forgotten them. He had intended to free them from bondage and God planned to direct Moses to lead the fight against Pharaoh and after that he would lead the Hebrew children out of Egypt, eventually leading them into a land of milk and honey (see Exodus 3:14-18).

God had now given Moses the job description. Is it no wonder that the man who was once run from Pharaoh failed, for in his mind he was just a poor shepherd who had lived in the backside of the desert for too many years. He was just like us, who deny God's ability to take us through, and thus shorten His arm. God wants us to trust Him and yet we are fearful. If we would only recognize that God is willing to help us! He cannot help us unless we are willing to believe and trust in Him. So often we only shake our heads and deny the power of God to solve the problem. Instead of looking to Him, we look at the problem, which increases in size every time we look at it. When will we finally realize that God's ability to aid us is fruitless without a demonstration of faith? (Read Matthew 13:54-58).

It is a fact of life. We must realize that if we believe on one hand that satan, the enemy of God, can bring us harm, then we open that door and he is able to do so. If, however, we accept that he is a defeated foe, that Jesus the Christ defeated him and won our great victory, then he is unable to harm us. I'm sure that God often wonders why we believe that His enemy can take control over our lives for harm, but we hesitate to believe that God Himself can benefit our lives by His great and wonderful power!

Moses was in a hard place. He had given up his life as a leader of men and God was calling him back into Egypt where he had once killed a man. It seemed plausible to him that the Hebrews knew about the killing, for after all, he had killed on their behalf. He wondered if they would now believe that God had sent him. *"And Moses answered and said, But, behold, they will not believe me, nor hearken unto my voice: for they will say, The Lord hath not appeared unto thee. And the Lord said unto him, What is that in thine hand? And he said, A rod. And he said, Cast it on the ground. And he cast it on the ground, and it became a serpent; and Moses fled from before it. And the Lord said unto Moses, Put forth thine hand, and take it by the tail. And he put forth his hand, and caught it, and it became a rod in his hand: That they may believe that the Lord God of their fathers, the God of Abraham, the God of Isaac, and the God of Jacob, hath appeared unto thee. And the Lord said furthermore unto him, Put now thine hand into thy bosom. And he put his hand into his bosom: and when he took it out, behold, his hand was leprous as snow. And he said, Put thine hand into thy bosom again. And he put his hand into his bosom again; and plucked it out of his bosom, and, behold, it was turned again as his other flesh" (Exodus 4:1-7).*

Those were most interesting signs that the Lord God showed Moses. First, when he threw down his shepherd's staff, was the point where his job title changed. Though he had picked up the staff and been a shepherd for many years, he would now be God's hand in the deliverance of the Hebrew children. And when his rod became a snake he fled from it. God called him back and told him to reach out his hand and to pick up the snake by its tail. In Egypt the snake was a deity. It was a great symbol of royal power and authority often used by Egyptian Pharaohs as a design to decorate their clothing and their crowns. When God commanded Moses to take the snake by the tail, in essence God was telling Moses that he would be the one who would cast down the royal heads of Egypt. When God showed Moses his leprous hand and then healed it, He was demonstrating that He, God, would give Moses power over all of the things that were to come against the Hebrew children and that Moses was to be His emissary and would be well-able to protect them and keep them safe. God showed him all of this to encourage him and build up his faith.

Moses still doubted his ability. He told the Lord something that the Lord already knew. He was not a good speaker. God then asked him, *who made your mouth?* (To read more, refer to Exodus 4:11-12). God was testing Moses because to do that which God wanted done would take faith, courage and determination. Again God told Moses, *"Go and I will be with your mouth, and I will teach you what to say."* Moses deferred and took no ownership of the job that was to be done. Finally the anger of the Lord was kindled against Moses. In frustration God told Moses that his brother, Aaron the Levite, was looking for him and he was to tell his brother all that God had said. God promised to be with both men and would put the words in their mouths, words that would overpower the majesty of all Egypt. Then Moses returned the sheep to his father-in-law and told him that he would be leaving to go back to Egypt. Then God spoke to him and told him that the men who sought his life were now dead. God knew that was bothering Moses all along, but He did not mention that it was no longer a problem and until Moses accepted the deal and was in total agreement with it.

Moses then returned to the land of Egypt and along the way the long-separated brothers finally met. One can only imagine the emotions of these two men, both being aware that this was a divine meeting and there was a call of God upon their lives. *"And Moses and Aaron went and gathered together all the elders of the children of Israel: And Aaron spake all the words which the Lord had spoken unto Moses, and did the signs in the sight of the people. And the people believed: and when they heard that the Lord had visited the children of Israel, and that he had looked upon their affliction, then they bowed their heads and worshipped"* (Exodus 4:29-31).

The scene was set, the combatants were in the land; the God of Israel was set to challenge Pharaoh, his gods, his magicians, his army and all his horses and chariots. This sounds kind of lopsided doesn't it? But that is the way the Lord God liked it. He liked it then and He likes it that way now. The Hebrew children, those who had faith to believe, would see the strong arm of the Lord miraculously move on their behalf. Their faith could not waver nor fail. Their very lives depended upon it.

The Battle is Joined

Moses and Aaron met with the elders and showed them the signs and wonders which God had given them. The elders bowed before God... a beautiful picture of God's chosen people accepting His wonderful plan. They had heard about Jehovah God all of their lives and they were hearing that His deliverance was at hand. What they had been hearing about for so many years was then becoming a reality. God was going to free His people but few understood the trials that lay ahead of them.

Soon after this meeting Moses and Aaron met with Pharaoh. They went in the power of the Lord and were rebuffed. They asked only for a few days in order to worship their God, and the King of Egypt said, *"...Who is the LORD, that I should obey his voice to let Israel go? (Exodus 5:2a).*

This certainly indicated that life was about to get tougher. Because of that simple request made by Moses and Aaron, Pharaoh's response came in the form of severe punishment against the Hebrew children. They would no longer be given straw to make bricks. They were forced to search for it; however, they still had to make their usual quota of bricks for the massive building projects of the Pharaohs. Their leaders went to Pharaoh to plead their case, but to no avail. There was no one to blame except Moses, so Moses went to the Lord and in a fashion blamed Him (see Exodus 5:20-23).

This was the beginning of the testing for Moses, Aaron, and the Hebrew children. Would they have the faith to carry them through this battle or would

they fail before they ever left Egypt? There would always be doubters and complainers, but the question remained, would the body survive the difficulties ahead?

Again God spoke and He said, *"...I am the Lord: And I appeared unto Abraham, unto Isaac, and unto Jacob, by the name of God Almighty, but by my name Jehovah was I not known to them. And I have also established my covenant with them, to give them the land of Canaan, the land of their pilgrimage, wherein they were strangers. And I have also heard the groaning of the children of Israel, whom the Egyptians keep in bondage; and I have remembered my covenant. Wherefore say unto the children of Israel, I am the Lord, and I will bring you out from under the burdens of the Egyptians, and I will rid you of their bondage, and I will redeem you with a stretched out arm, and with great judgments: And I will take you to me for a people, and I will be to you a God: and ye shall know that I am the Lord your God, which bringeth you out from under the burdens of the Egyptians. And I will bring you in unto the land, concerning the which I did swear to give it to Abraham, to Isaac, and to Jacob; and I will give it to you for an heritage: I am the Lord"* (Exodus 6:2-8). One would think that this declaration would be enough, but the children of Israel would not hear it. Moses had to face Pharaoh again. He dreaded going back to Pharaoh but God told him to make the commands. God also told Moses that He, God, would harden Pharaoh's heart.

There will be times in our walk with God when what He tells us to do may make no sense at all. Why would He send us to do a tough job when He already knows that the outcome will not be successful? After we have walked with Him for a number of years, questions such as these will make most of us smile. We have learned that whatever God does, and whatever He asks of us, He has a plan and purpose for it all, and His plan is for good, our good and to His glory. In time we will grow to understand His ways.

God wanted Moses and Aaron to return to Pharaoh in order to begin the great judgments that God was to bring against Egypt, its gods and its people. The big show was about to begin and neither man nor beast would ever be the same again.

Moses and Aaron returned to confront Pharaoh. God had directed them, and they were faithful to do all that God had required. Before Pharaoh and his officials, Aaron threw down his rod. As before, it again became a snake. Pharaoh called for his magicians who threw down their rods and their rods became snakes. There was one big difference though; Aaron's rod swallowed the rods of the magicians. This they could not duplicate no matter how hard they tried. They should have understood that this so called ignorant Jew had just demonstrated that the gods of Egypt would soon become subject to the God of Israel. God had just begun His assault against the gods of the powerful nation of Egypt. He was going to prove that no matter what, He was God Jehovah, and He was going to break their power and influence. God would have the day; no matter that Pharaoh's heart was hardened and that he would not let them go.

Again they appeared before Pharaoh. It was the morning and the usual time for Pharaoh to walk to the Great Nile and worship. The Nile was mother to all who lived in Egypt. People worshiped her, and took their livelihood from her banks and from her waters. When Pharaoh arrived he saw Moses, and when he refused to listen, Moses raised his staff and all of the water in the Nile turned to blood. Not just in the river but also all of its branches, canals, cisterns, and reservoirs. Then the fish died, the water stank, and no one could take a drink from her. Upon seeing this, Pharaoh turned and went into his house with his heart still as hard as ever.

Turning the water to blood was but the first of the miracles that God would use to free His people. The second miracle also had to do with the Nile. One of the earliest forms of idolatry was the worship of frogs. So Moses called forth frogs, millions and millions of frogs. The frogs were everywhere; they were outside, inside and even in the bed of Pharaoh. Moses gave him an ultimatum that, if he would let them go and worship their God, then Moses would call off the frogs. To this proposal Pharaoh agreed so God killed off the frogs. They died and were stacked up in great piles, and they stank. And Pharaoh recanted.

Next came the lice. At God's instruction Aaron smote the land with his rod and out of the dust of the land came lice, a small insect which was scarcely visible, but which penetrated everywhere and caused great distress. Many times the magicians tried to duplicate the work that they were seeing done by the Israelites, but they were unable to stand against Moses, Aaron and their God. They finally admitted to Pharaoh that the finger of God was really doing this. Again, Pharaoh's heart was hardened.

These great plagues came in groups of three and the next three plagues would come without Moses and Aaron. God, Himself, would prove to all that He was the One who was bringing these plagues. He had drawn a line in the sand of Egypt and would come against Pharaoh and all his gods.

Now God sent Moses to speak to Pharaoh and tell him once again to let His people go. If he would not listen, God would personally send swarms of flies upon him, his household, and the houses of his people, and on all the ground around them. He would come against the land with flies; however, He would protect the houses of the Hebrew children. He would put a boundary around His people. The Hebrews shall not suffer from the biting flies that He would send against Egyptians. Pharaoh would not listen so God sent the flies. He sent grievous swarms of flies into the house of Pharaoh, into his servant's houses and into all of Egypt; no one could work or rest for the land was covered with flies. This time Pharaoh called for Moses and told him to go and sacrifice unto your his God in the land. Moses could not accept that offer because God had given them specific instructions about where they were to worship; they were to go three days' journey into the wilderness, and sacrifice unto the Lord as He had commanded. Pharaoh agreed and he entreated Moses to ask God to remove the flies. Moses did, God did, and Pharaoh's heart was again hardened.

Once again God sent Moses back to Pharaoh. This time God promised that if Pharaoh would not let His people go, then He, God, would bring upon the nation of Egypt grievous murrain. This is a highly infectious disease, a terrible plague that was to come against the Egyptian cattle, horses, asses, oxen, sheep and camels. God also promised that He would separate the cattle of the Hebrew children from this plague. He gave a set time in which this disease would come. He gave Pharaoh every opportunity to call this thing off; all he had to do was repent. Pharaoh did nothing to deter the attack, so the murrain came and all the cattle of Egypt died. Pharaoh sent a spy to check out the cattle of the Hebrews; and it was reported to him that they were very much alive. Pharaoh's heart was hardened and again he refused to allow the Hebrews to go.

It is interesting to notice that though God included horses, asses, and camels in the list of those who could be subject to the murrain, He only took the cattle. Could it be because God knew that Pharaoh would need his horses, asses, and camels so that his army would be able to chase after the Israelites, and then drown in the sea? God does plan ahead!

It is also important to note that though God could have destroyed all the Egyptians, God Himself said that He would not destroy them so that they would not disappear from the face of the earth, so that God's name should be declared across all the earth. That thankfully gives us the history we are presently enjoying.

Then God instructed Moses to take handfuls of ash from the furnace and in the sight of Pharaoh sprinkle the ash toward heaven. Moses did this and immediately the skin of each man was covered in boils. This fell upon men and beasts. Egyptian magicians could not even try to duplicate what Moses had done because they too were covered with boils. But Pharaoh's heart remained hard even after this great move of God.

God then told Moses to approach Pharaoh again and told him that since he had exalted himself against His people and would not let them go to worship their God, then He would bring a grievous rain against Egypt. It would be a rain like no other, because in truth, it would be a rain of hail. Never had there been such hail as that which came against them then. This hail came down upon every man and beast that was found in the field and they all died.

There had been some Egyptians who had saved their cattle from the murrain because they believed in what the God of Israel had said, and they who regarded the word of the Lord a second time brought their animals into their houses against the hail.

Then the Lord told Moses to stretch forth his hand toward heaven that there may be hail in the land. Moses obeyed and the Lord sent thunder and hail, and there was fire that ran along the ground. Nothing like it had ever been seen in the land of Egypt since it had become a nation. Devastation was everywhere; every man, and animal that had not found shelter was dead, every herb was destroyed, and every tree was broken down. Also the flax and barley were smitten. Only in the land of Goshen, the home of the Hebrew children, had they been without hail.

Now Pharaoh sent for Moses and Aaron. He admitted that he had sinned; he acknowledged that he and his people were wicked and the Lord alone was righteous. He asked that they entreat the Lord and asked that there be no more thundering and hail. Pharaoh quickly agreed to allow the children of God freedom to go and worship Him. Moses responded to Pharaoh by saying, *"As soon as I am gone out of the city, I will spread abroad my hands unto the Lord; and the thunder shall cease, neither shall there be any more hail; that thou mayest know how that the earth is the Lord's"* (Exodus 9:29). He also explained to Pharaoh this had been done so that Pharaoh would realize that all the earth belonged to the Lord. Moses walked out of the city and raised his hands unto the Lord and the thunder and hail ceased and the rain no longer poured upon the land. And when Pharaoh saw that the thunder, the hail and rain ceased then his heart was hardened as well as those of his servants.

Again Moses and Aaron went to Pharaoh, they gave him God's message that if Pharaoh would not obey to let the people go to worship Him then God would send an army of locusts. There would be so many locusts that they would make the earth disappear from sight, and they would eat everything that remained upon the earth, all that was left from the damaging hail. He also said that the locusts would fill Pharaoh's houses, his servants' houses and all the houses of the Egyptians. The only ones to escape would be the children of God. Moses turned and walked away from Pharaoh, and his servants cried out to let the Hebrews go or else the servants would be totally destroyed. Pharaoh called for Moses and Aaron and told them to go serve their Lord. He then asked who would be going with them.

Moses said everyone would go… the young and the old, the sons and the daughters, the flocks and the herds. All would go to worship God. Pharaoh then suggested that the little ones should stay lest any harm should come upon them. Moses refused because he knew what Pharaoh really meant, that the children would be held as hostages to insure the return of the Hebrews. Then he and Aaron were driven out from Pharaoh's presence.

At that point God told Moses to stretch out his hand over the land of Egypt and He would send the locusts. Moses raised his hand and a strong east wind came and it brought with it many locusts. They covered the face of the whole earth so that the earth was darkened and they ate everything that the hail had left. Then in haste, Pharaoh called for Moses and Aaron, he again confessed that he had sinned, and he asked that God would take away the locusts. Moses went out and asked the Lord, and He turned the east wind westward and the locusts were sent to the Red Sea. There was not one living locust remaining in all the land of Egypt. But the Lord hardened Pharaoh's heart again and he would not let the Hebrew children go to worship their God.

Then the Lord told Moses to stretch out his hand and there would be thick darkness over all the land of Egypt. It was a darkness that they could feel as it settled upon them. Some believed that this was a severe sand storm that God had called upon them. They could neither see nor walk, they could not move from their places nor did they know what was happening to them. It lasted for three long days and nights. But in the land of Goshen there was light. Pharaoh called Moses. He would allow the children of God to leave, but he asked that the flocks remain as a pledge that they would return. Moses told Pharaoh that leaving the flocks was not an option because they would need them for sacrifices unto the Lord. Moses said that not a hoof would remain, they would all go. Again the Lord had hardened Pharaoh's heart. As Moses turned to leave, Pharaoh affirmed that Moses would not see Pharaoh again, to which Moses agreed. They were coming to the final climax and Moses knew from conversations with God that he would never see Pharaoh again. (See Exodus 10:27-29).

God had indeed spoken to Moses and He made clear to Moses that this was to be the last plague and the time for the Hebrew children, His chosen bride, to be released by Pharaoh. He had told Moses what he was intending to do and that midnight was to be the time when the final strike of God would come against the Egyptians.

God then advised Moses to speak to the Hebrews and suggest to them that they should borrow from their neighbors because God was giving them favor. The Egyptians freely gave to them all that they had in silver and gold. We have often heard about the multiple fold return, which God would call for on behalf of His children. The return of all the silver and gold from the Egyptians is a fine demonstration of this law because most of this treasure originally came from Jacob when he first moved his family into Egypt. He had been a very rich man and somehow throughout the years the Egyptians had taken his wealth. But now God was calling for it to come back, multiplied, into the hands of the Hebrew children so that when they went out they went as victors, no longer as slaves. He was continually preparing and improving His bride. The study about the ancient Hebrew weddings reveals this gift of gold came as a proper wedding gift from God to His beloved Bride.

God had told Moses that at midnight He, God, would go out into the midst of Egypt, and all of the firstborn in the land of Egypt would die. From the firstborn of Pharaoh to the firstborn of the lowliest maid, and also the firstborn of every beast, all would die. And God said there would be a great cry throughout the land of Egypt like never before. God also said that against any of the children of Israel there would be not a sound, not even the sound of a dog moving his tongue. Israel would again see that God had made a difference between the Hebrew children and the Egyptians.

Then the God of Israel instructed Moses about the night of the great Passover. God also changed the order of the calendar; from that day forth, the Passover night became the beginning of the year. It is also interesting to note that in Exodus 12:3 God called Israel a congregation for the very first time; He was changing this loose assortment and configuration of people into a solid congregation with Him as the only head. He also instructed that in every man's house there be a lamb in its first year of life without blemish. It must be selected on the tenth day of the month and reserved until the fourteenth day of the same month. Then the whole congregation of Israel on the evening of the fourteenth day would kill the lambs. Then they would take of the blood of the innocent lambs and strike it against the two side posts and the upper lintel of the doorway of each home. Then they would eat the flesh of the lamb that night.

The Hebrews were also instructed as to the cooking of the lamb. Usually their meat was cooked by boiling and the meat was called sodden, but this night would be different and the meat was to be roasted quickly. It was to be eaten with unleavened bread and bitter herbs. Everything was to be consumed; nothing was to be left for the morrow and if perchance there was some left, then it was to be burned with fire.

They were also instructed how to dress for the evening meal. They were to have their loins girded, sandals on their feet, and their staff in their hands, and they were to eat in haste because it was the Lord's Passover.

God also instructed them that this would be a memorial, a yearly feast, and an ordinance that would stand forever in Hebrew worship. He also instructed them in the cleansing of their houses from leaven and in the eating for seven days of unleavened bread. This time of eating the unleavened bread would always be unto them a sign of remembrance of the time in which God redeemed them from Egypt. And when the youngest would ask why we celebrate, we ought to tell them of all that God has done through all generations on our behalf. When Moses finished telling them all that God had told him, then the people bowed their heads in worship.

And it came to pass that just as God had said, the Lord smote all the firstborn in the land of Egypt, man and beast He killed, but He passed over the houses of the Hebrews, which held the telltale sign of innocent blood. Pharaoh called for both Moses and Aaron, and told them to rise up and go from among his people. He told them to go and serve the Lord, to take their flocks and their herds and be gone. He also added something amazing. Pharaoh asked for God's blessing.

So the people of Israel took their kneading troughs with them, wrapped up in their clothing and set high upon their shoulders. They walked out of Egypt taking all that they owned, their flocks, their herds and their gold and silver; there was no opposition, just the sounds of weeping in their ears. The Hebrew children had sojourned in the Land of Egypt for exactly 430 years when the Lord their God delivered them and took them out to be His bride.

Some people might find all of these plagues excessive but God wanted His children released to Him. He also wanted them never to forget the trouble that He had gone to and the power that He had used in order to set them free. He explained to Moses that he was hardening Pharaoh's heart and even those of his servants so that one day the Jews would recall these events word-by-word and plague-by-plague.

If perchance we have Jewish friends and acquaintances in our lives, and for any of us who have ever been invited to a

Seder meal during the Passover season, then we know that even today they worship God while they relive each and every event of this story. During that celebration of the Seder meal in which they relive their great liberation from Egypt they will sing a song that explains their gratitude to God for their freedom. The special Hebrew word in the song is Dayenu (Die-a-new), which means, it would have been enough.

Dayenu

"If He had brought us out of Egypt, and not executed judgment against the Egyptians, - Dayenu, it would have sufficed us!

If He had executed judgment against the Egyptians, and not against their idols,
- Dayenu, it would have sufficed us!

If He had executed judgment against their idols, and not smitten their firstborn,
- Dayenu, it would have sufficed us!

If He had smitten their firstborn, and not given us their wealth,
- Dayenu, it would have sufficed us!

If He had not given us their wealth, and not split the sea for us,
- Dayenu, it would have sufficed us!"

These are interesting words in this song. However, these things were not enough; nothing God promised or accomplished would ever totally suffice the Hebrew children, these whom God wanted as His Bride.

The Departure from Egypt

And it came to pass that Pharaoh had indeed let the Hebrews go to worship their God. They left Egypt and made their way to the Red Sea. God could have taken them a much shorter route, but then they would have immediately faced the warriors of the Philistines who even the Egyptians could not defeat. He also knew that when things got tough there would be those who would want to return to Egypt. So God led His people, a cloud by day and a pillar of fire by night. He turned the people to appear as if they were going southward and Pharaoh surmised incorrectly that they had been caught up in nets that were left by fishermen, and would be easy prey for his great armies. However, God had deliberately led them to encamp in a place that was between Migdol, a city of the delta, and the Red Sea.

While Israel was following God, Pharaoh, with hope of reclaiming the Jews, gathered his mighty army together. Six hundred well-armed men, horses and chariots, comprised a formidable sight for any army to face, let alone the untrained Hebrew men, women and children who appeared to have lost their way in the wilderness.

It might have been the rays of the setting sun that fell upon the spears of the approaching Egyptian army that quickly turned the Hebrew children's hearts from thanksgiving to fear. Upon seeing the Egyptians fully arrayed for battle, their courage failed and they anticipated an imminent attack. Then, of course, they turned against Moses and Aaron for bringing them into the wilderness to die.

We all know there are times in our lives that seem so overwhelming that we think even God cannot help us. This was certainly one of these times for the Hebrews. Instead of falling on their faces before Him they looked at the geography and figured that all was lost. They never even thought about the fact that God was with them and that He had recently shown them many signs and wonders. Doubt ruled the day for them, and Moses said unto the people, *"...Fear ye not, stand still, and see the salvation of the* Lord, *which he will shew to you to day: for the Egyptians whom ye have seen to day, ye shall see them again no more for ever. The* Lord *shall fight for you, and ye shall hold your peace"* (Exodus 14:13-14).

So Moses did what God told him. He lifted up his staff and stretched out his hand to divide the sea. Israel began to cross the Red Sea upon dry ground. So God went across before the camp of Israel and when they were about halfway across the sea He turned to follow after them. So it was God Himself Who came between the camp of Israel and the armies of Egypt. He was a light unto the Hebrew children and darkness to the Egyptians, and in that darkness Pharaoh and his army became confused. When all the Hebrews had safely crossed over the Red Sea then Moses stretched out his hand over the sea and the water flooded back and covered Pharaoh, his army, his horses and his chariots. The enemies of God were defeated and His Bride was redeemed. And His people saw all that He had done and they feared Him and His awesome power.

So God brought His Bride safely out of Egypt. Record books indicate that God led, with women and children added, at least two million people. That is no small feat considering that when Jacob took his family to Egypt, he brought with him only his sons, daughters, children and servants. This great exodus from Egypt was 430 years later and had become millions. God had saved them and brought them out from under the control of the Egyptians. It is marvelous to see that they left not in defeat but in triumph. Many look upon the departure of the Hebrew children from Egypt as a type of salvation, perhaps even an image of the promised Jesus, Son of the living God.

For those of us who are studying this story about God the Groom with His wedding planner, we see how He led His chosen Bride from their home, safely through the mikvah, a bath in the Red Sea. The mikvah is a part of the ancient wedding ceremony. Some scholars believe they went through a sort of baptism as they crossed through the Sea. However, water baptism is not mentioned in the Old Testament. When first mentioned it was at the hands of John the Baptist, who was a cousin to Jesus.

As in all Jewish weddings there are moments of great rejoicing. We have seen God's miraculous deliverance for His bride. Once they had safely crossed the sea, they turned and watched the sea close its gates and drown their pagan enemies. Then Miriam the prophetess and sister of Aaron, took a timbrel in her hand and began to dance and sing about the great triumph of God in which He rescued the Hebrew children. Their pursuers were all drowned in the sea.

The Travel unto Sinai

With the song of triumph still ringing in their ears the first part of the book of Exodus ends. According to Alfred Edersheim in his wonderful book of *Bible History Old Testament*, "Israel had now become a nation." Israel was God's chosen nation and He had just delivered all 2,000,000 of them from Egypt and was about to take them on their longest recorded walk. The second part of Exodus tells that story.

They now looked to the wilderness of Shur (Exodus 15:22), which is translated "the wall", and this was the path they would follow all the way to the Sinai. They would traverse the Sinai Peninsula, which extends between the Gulf of Suez on the west, and the Gulf of Akaba on the east. This arid land was marked with wadis, dry riverbeds, and these were the safest places for them to walk during the dry season. Every once in a while they would see evidence of the work of men, as Egyptians had at one time dug in the land for copper, iron and turquoise. And of course they would see the work of nature.

Springs of fresh water were scarce and scripture reminds us that they tried to buy food and water from the Edomites (Deuteronomy 2:6). Surely they sought help from the many passing caravans.

Scripture notes that they walked three days in the wilderness and found no water. They finally came to a place called Marah. Here the water was plentiful, but because of nitrate that leeched out of the surrounding ground, the water was very bitter.

Our pastor, Jamie Buckingham, taught us that the bitter water was a purgative and that once consumed

would cleanse their bodies of the fine foods of Egypt. God wanted them to drink the bitter water which would pass through them taking with it all of the memories of the food and drink that they had left behind. But they would not drink until God made the water sweet. He had taken them out of Egypt and now He wanted to take Egypt out of them; but they complained and refused to drink. Once again they refused God's plan, so God showed Moses how to turn the bitter water into sweet water and then the people drank. But because they would not drink the bitter water they continued to hearken back to the foods of Egypt, which were always on their mind. Once again they disobeyed God and for the rest of the trip, 40 years, He patiently listened to all their complaining (Read Exodus 15:22-25).

It was at Marah that God said to Moses, *"...If thou wilt diligently hearken to the voice of the LORD thy God, and wilt do that which is right in his sight, and wilt give ear to his commandments, and keep all his statutes, I will put none of these diseases upon thee, which I have brought upon the Egyptians: for I am the LORD that healeth thee"* (Exodus 15:26).

It has been recorded that their first camping place was at Elim. That area was well known by those who traveled there as a bountiful supply of water and shade. The Hebrews could rest comfortably there.

Then they continued their journey and they came into the wilderness of Sin that is between Elim and the Sinai. This is one of the most desolate places in the entire wilderness area. It was in this inhospitable desert that the children of Israel began to murmur against Moses and Aaron. They said in Exodus 16:3, *"...Would to God we had died by the hand of the LORD in the land of Egypt, when we sat by the flesh pots, and when we did eat bread to the full; for ye have brought us forth into this wilderness, to kill this whole assembly with hunger."*

Exodus 16:4-5 tells us, *"Then said the Lord unto Moses, Behold, I will rain bread from heaven for you; and the people shall go out and gather a certain rate every day, that I may prove them, whether they will walk in my law, or no. And it shall come to pass, that on the sixth day they shall prepare that which they bring in; and it shall be twice as much as they gather daily."*

Exodus 16:6-7, *"And Moses and Aaron said unto all the children of Israel, At even, then ye shall know that the Lord hath brought you out from the land of Egypt: And in the morning, then ye shall see the glory of the Lord; for that he heareth your murmurings against the Lord: and what are we, that ye murmur against us?"* This is remarkable, hard for the Bible reader to truly comprehend. How was it that the Hebrew children needed yet another sign to prove that God Himself was their deliverer? He had shown them so many mighty signs and miracles that could have been done only by His Hand. His love for, and patience with, this ungrateful mob was overwhelming. They seldom accepted Him for who He was. When He blessed them they were never really satisfied... a truly thankless bunch!

However, God was about to show them another great sign. Aaron then spoke to the congregation and told them that God would appear and His glory would come before them as a cloud. Then God spoke to Moses and told him that He, God, had heard the murmurings of the children of Israel so now He would send them another sign. He said to tell them that by evening they would eat flesh and in the morning they would be filled with bread. Then they would know that He was Lord.

All that He said came to pass. In the evening, quail came up and covered the camp. There was no difficulty catching them because they landed in their hands and at their feet. They asked for meat so He gave it to them. They also asked for bread, so in the morning once the dew was lifted upon the face of the wilderness there was a covering of small white round flakes that looked like a coriander seed. Moses told them that this was the bread which the Lord had given them to eat. Then Moses gave them instructions about harvesting the manna that had come from God. They were to gather in the morning just enough for every man according to the number in his tent. Some gathered more and some gathered less. Those who had gathered less had enough and those who had gathered more had enough. In God's supply there was nothing left over nor was there any lack! Moses had told them not to save any manna for the next day but true to course those who had been disobedient found the manna that they had saved bred worms and stank.

Moses also told them that harvesting the manna was a work for the morning because when the sun came out then the manna would melt away. They were also directed that at the day of preparation for the Sabbath (Shabbat), which would be the Friday immediately before the Sabbath, they were to gather enough to last them through two days. They would then bake and seethe the extra manna so that it could be used safely for the morning and through that day. The Lord had made these preparations since the Jews were not allowed to do any servile work on the Shabbat day, which was Saturday, as we know it. Every Shabbat, Saturday, was and still is a holy day as it was a day for total rest. By God's provision they could save the manna for that day without any fear of it becoming wormy.

This manna was a wonderful miraculous provision by God; He made it and fed it to the Hebrew children. It was a heavenly corn, the food of the angels, and it was His creation. He provided it for to them for the forty years that they would live in the wilderness. It was a substance so special to God that He told Moses to save an Omer measure of manna. It was to be kept safe in order to show the generations who would follow that God had fed His Bride with heavenly bread through the forty years of the wilderness experience.

Alfred Edersheim, in his book on *Bible History Old Testament* wrote, "That Presence, the visible presence of God, ought to have prevented their murmurings, or rather changed it into prayer and praise. And so it always is, that, before God supplies our wants, He shows us that His presence has been near, and He reveals His glory. That presence is in itself sufficient; for no good thing shall be wanting to them that trust in Him." And he continues on page 196. "Thus, alike in the *rain of bread from heaven,* in the ordinance of its ingathering, and in the Sabbath law of its sanctified use, did God prove Israel – even as He now proves us: whether we will 'walk in His law or no' (See Exodus 16:4).

It was time for the Hebrew children to move on. So the congregation moved from the wilderness of Sin. After their journey, they were led to pitch in Rephidim (Refi-deem), but it was a place without water. It was a wide plain surrounded by rocky hills and mountains but it was a very dry place. The people chided Moses and demanded water. They complained and sang the old familiar song; why did you bring us out of Egypt to kill us along with our children and our cattle? Moses cried unto the Lord. His plea was in earnest because they were about to stone him.

God answered Moses and told him to take the rod which had divided the sea, and take the elders, and then He said, *Behold, I will stand before thee there upon the rock in Horeb (Exodus 17:6), which means dry and parched.* Moses then heard God tell him to smite the rock and there shall water come out of it, that the people may drink. And Moses did so in the presence of the elders of Israel, and out of the rock gushed clean, clear water. This was indeed a rock in a hard place, but once again the Lord our God found water for His children. He was faithful to take care of them but no sooner had their thirsts been quenched did trouble arise. As the last of the stragglers appeared to quench their thirst a band of warriors from the tribe of Amalek appeared. God called this a cowardly and wicked deed as recorded in Deuteronomy 25:18, also noting that Israel had no real way to protect herself.

Amalek was a relative, as they were descendants of Esau. They were the first fruit of the heathens and were the sworn enemies of God. This is the first recorded attack by the kingdoms of this world against the children of God. If we look at the day in which we live we can see that this hatred between the kingdoms of the world and the Kingdom of God has roots that run deep in the hearts of the Middle Eastern people. Moses told Joshua to choose men to go out the next day and fight against Amalek and he, Moses, would stand on the hill with the rod of God in his hand. Joshua did as Moses had commanded; Moses took with him Aaron and Hur and he went to the top of the hill. It came to pass, when Moses held up his hand, that Israel prevailed: and when He let down his hand, Amalek prevailed (Read Exodus 17:11). Moses' hands became heavy so they took a stone and he sat upon it while Aaron and Hur held up his hands and his hands remained steady until the sun went down. Joshua defeated Amalek with the edge of the sword. *"And the LORD said unto Moses, Write this for a memorial in a book, and rehearse it in the ears of Joshua: for I will utterly put out the remembrance of Amalek from under heaven" (Exodus 17:14).* And Moses built an altar and called the name of it, Jehovah-nissi, the Lord my banner, for the rod of God had been their banner that day. And he said, *"...Because the Lord hath sworn that the Lord will have war with Amalek from generation to generation" (Exodus 17:16).* In this statement, God is telling us that as long as Israel has enemies, He will be there to help her. She is still His beloved and as we look at the world today we see the enemies of Israel are ever-growing and becoming more numerous than ever before. However, we need not worry because God will prevail. No matter what the sons or daughters of Amalek shall do, God Himself has sworn that the plans of men to bring war against Israel, will indeed mean war against Him. Israel is His, and He will be their banner again and again, forever and ever. Amen!

After the Hebrew children recognized and acknowledged their victory against Amalek they departed that area and finally made camp in the wilderness of Sinai. They set their camp before the great mountain where God was to meet with them in a most personal and powerful way.

God Prepared His People and They Became His Bride

The Hebrew people were about to become a Covenant nation. God called Moses to meet with Him high upon the great mountain named Sinai. Moses went up to God and the Lord God said, *"Thus shalt thou say to the house of Jacob, and tell the children of Israel; Ye have seen what I did unto the Egyptians, and how I bare you on eagles' wings, and brought you unto myself. Now therefore, if ye will obey my voice indeed, and keep my covenant, then ye shall be a peculiar treasure unto me above all people: for all the earth is mine: And ye shall be unto me a kingdom of priests, and an holy nation. These are the words which thou shalt speak unto the children of Israel"* (Exodus 19:3b-6).

Moses came down from the mountain and he called all the elders to him. He was still acting as the groomsman for God as he laid before them all that the Lord had said and they answered that they would do as God willed. They, for the moment, were in full agreement with God. And Moses returned to God bearing the words of the people. God told Moses that He would come to meet him in a thick cloud so that the people would be able to hear His conversation with Moses and by so doing the people would truly believe that Moses had heard from God. Moses then told God that the children of Israel were in agreement with the plan and they would be in total obedience.

The Lord then told Moses to sanctify the people this day and the next, for on that day the Lord would come down on Mount Sinai and come into the sight of all the people. So Moses, following God's instructions, told them to sanctify themselves. In other words, they were to make themselves pure and holy before God by the ritual washing of their bodies. They refrained from contact with their wives or any other woman, and finally they washed all their garments so that they could stand clean before the Lord God. This was their second mikvah, but this one was wet. Moses then had barriers set all around the mountain and gave warning to the people that they could not pass the barriers nor touch the mountain, not even the very foot of the mountain, lest they would die. Man or beast, he said, would surely die.

And it came to pass that on the morning of the third day the mountain was covered in a thick heavy cloud that was filled with thunder and lightning. Then came the sound of the trumpet, the shofar (show-far), and it was exceedingly loud and all the people in the camp trembled. Moses then brought the people out of the camp to meet with God. Mount Sinai was altogether covered in smoke like the smoke of a furnace, because the Lord descended upon it and the whole mountain quaked greatly. Again the trumpet sounded and waxed louder and louder, Moses then spoke and God answered him using His own voice. And the Lord descended upon the top of the mount and he called Moses to come up and Moses did as the Lord required.

Out of this meeting with God came the beloved Ten Commandments. They are the beginning principles upon which all Jewish law is based. The first four commandments deal with reverence for God directly, while the latter six refer to man's relationship with his fellow man. The Jews call them the Ten Words and had they kept all these commandments faithfully, Israel would have lived forever in the perfect favor of God. God himself spoke the words and then wrote them on two tablets of stone. Refer to Exodus 20:1-17 *"And God spake all these words, saying,*

Vs. 2 I am the Lord *thy God, which have brought thee out of the land of Egypt, out of the house of bondage.*

Vs. 3 Thou shalt have no other gods before me.

Vs. 4 Thou shalt not make unto thee any graven image, or any likeness of any thing that is in heaven above, or that is in the earth beneath, or that is in the water under the earth.

Vs. 5 Thou shalt not bow down thyself to them, nor serve them: for I the Lord *thy God am a jealous God, visiting the iniquity of the fathers upon the children unto the third and fourth generation of them that hate me;*

Vs. 6 And shewing mercy unto thousands of them that love me, and keep my commandments.

Vs. 7 Thou shalt not take the name of the Lord *thy God in vain; for the* Lord *will not hold him guiltless that taketh his name in vain.*

Vs. 8 Remember the sabbath day, to keep it holy.

Vs. 9 Six days shalt thou labour, and do all thy work:

Vs. 10 But the seventh day is the sabbath of the Lord *thy God: in it thou shalt not do any work, thou, nor thy son, nor thy daughter, thy manservant, nor thy maidservant, nor thy cattle, nor thy stranger that is within thy gates:*

Vs. 11 For in six days the Lord *made heaven and earth, the sea, and all that in them is, and rested the seventh day: wherefore the* Lord *blessed the sabbath day, and hallowed it.*

Vs. 12 Honour thy father and thy mother: that thy days may be long upon the land which the Lord *thy God giveth thee.*

Vs. 13 Thou shalt not kill.

Vs. 14 Thou shalt not commit adultery.

Vs. 15 Thou shalt not steal.

Vs. 16 Thou shalt not bear false witness against thy neighbour.

Vs. 17 Thou shalt not covet thy neighbour's house, thou shalt not covet thy neighbour's wife, nor his manservant, nor his maidservant, nor his ox, nor his ass, nor any thing that is thy neighbour's."

While God spoke to Moses the people became fearful and slowly backed away from the sounds of the trumpet, the lightning, and the smoking mountain. When Moses came down to speak to the people they told him that they were willing to speak to and hear from him but they wanted no more direct communication with God. Moses responded that God only wanted to prove Himself to His people. But they were not willing, and stood afar off from God and his smoking mountain.

Then God gave them a series of diverse laws, judgments and ordinances, He gave the Hebrew people directions by which to live their lives. If they would follow the directions they could live blessed lives. If they would believe God and follow Him then God's favor would forever be theirs. What God gave them begins at Exodus 21 and goes on through Exodus 23.

The glory of the Lord lived upon the great mountain and clouds of fire descended upon it. It was as if the mountain was covered by fire and on the occasions when Moses went up in obedience to God, he would disappear into the fire. Moses would be there alone with God for forty days and forty nights.

During that time God gave Moses the tablets of stone on which He Himself had written the Ten Commandments. He also gave Moses instructions for the offering to be given for the building of the tabernacle, which was to be their place of worship. This tabernacle would be carried with them for the rest of their forty-year journey. God gave instructions for the making of the curtains, the altar and the veil. He taught Moses about the consecration of Aaron and his sons who would be the priests of the tabernacle. He designed their priestly clothing. God also including directions for the making of the Urim and the Thummim, the special breastplate that would be worn over the heart of Aaron the high priest. He taught them the rites of consecration and the burnt offering and the altar of incense. He also taught Moses how to make the holy anointing oil and how to keep the Sabbath. All of these things did God teach Moses while he was there with Him on the mountain for 40 days and 40 nights.

But what were the Hebrew children doing while Moses was with God? They became impatient and wanted Aaron to make them a god. He did this using the gold that the Egyptians had given them by the hand of God. Aaron melted some of the gold and formed a calf and built an altar before it. Aaron made a feeble attempt trying to remind them that it was God Who had brought them out of Egypt and reminded them by saying, *Tomorrow is a feast to the Lord.* But the next day they rose up and brought offerings to the calf of gold. Then they sat down to eat and drink, and rose up to play. The Lord God said to Moses, *"... Go, get thee down; for thy people, which thou broughtest out of the land of Egypt, have corrupted themselves:" (Exodus 32:7)*.

Now we have a wonderful example of the love that Moses had for the Hebrew people, because God in His anger wanted to destroy all of the Hebrew children, His chosen race, and His selected bride. Moses stood before God and pleaded for the safekeeping of the people. Moses told Him that the Egyptians would say that God had delivered them out of Egypt in order to destroy them. Moses then reminded Him of His promise to Abraham, Isaac, and Israel, that He would multiply their seed into a great nation. *"And the LORD repented of the evil which he thought to do unto his people" (Exodus 32:14).* Imagine having that sort of conversation with God!

Moses came down the mountain with the sounds of the celebration by the Hebrews in his ears. In his hands he had the tablets of stone, which carried the commandments, written by the finger of God. Moses knew that this was not the sound of fearful men but the singing of revelers who had indeed corrupted themselves, and who now stood naked before Him. Moses cast down the tablets of stone and they broke against the base of the mountain. Moses then confronted Aaron and In a manner, Aaron blamed the people. Then Moses stood at the gate of the camp and asked, who is on the Lord's side? That day about three thousand men died. Moses told the Hebrew children that their sin was great and that he would return to God and make atonement for them. God heard Moses but nevertheless promised that one day He would visit their sin upon them which of course He did. It became clear in Exodus 32:34-35 when we read about God's final judgment upon those who worshiped the golden calf.

Moses took a tent, some think that it was his own tent, and pitched it out from camp and he called it the tent of meeting. When Moses first entered into the tent then the cloudy pillar, which was the Lord, descended and the Lord spoke with Moses. They spoke face to face as one friend to another. The people saw the cloudy pillar at the tent door and all the people rose up and worshiped. God promised that His presence would stay with them and that He would give them rest. Now Moses asked of God a personal gift. He asked to see the presence of His glory. And the Lord God denied him the right to see his face, however, He did allow him to see His backside. Moses stood in the cleft of the rock and God covered him with His hand as He walked by, then God removed His hand and Moses saw what no other man has ever seen, the backside of God.

God also instructed Moses to cut out two new tablets like the first ones that he destroyed. Moses arose early in the morning and went up the mountain as God had instructed him and took in his hand the two tablets of stone. At this time God announced to Moses that He would make a covenant with the nation of Israel. He had never made covenant with any other people and to this day that covenant with Israel still stands. This is the marriage covenant between God and the nation of Israel. God spoke these words to Moses as He would to a friend and Moses bowed before Him and worshiped Him. Moses wrote down all the words of this great covenant and He called it the Book of the Covenant. These words can be found in Exodus 20-23. God still favors those marvelous words that He spoke to Moses so many years ago.

It is good to take note how precisely God followed the ancient Israeli wedding plan. We have seen how God brought the Hebrew children to their betrothal in Egypt. At their departure He gave them gifts of gold, on through the Red Sea as a dry mikvah and then beyond. Now at Mount Sinai, He gave His bride a ketubah, bearing the words of the commandments and His ordinances and laws that served as His promises to keep them. And then He gave them the marriage covenant with its seal of blood.

In Exodus 24:3 Moses read to the people the marriage covenant written by God and the people answered with one voice, *"All the words which the Lord hath said will we do."* This is agreement, much like saying, "I do!"

In the morning Moses rose and built an altar according to the instructions of God. He built it with twelve pillars, one for each of the tribes of the Hebrew people. Each tribe was in agreement and they brought burnt offerings and peace offerings before God. When the sacrifice had been made then Moses took half of the blood of the covenant and sprinkled it on the altar and then he read again the Covenant with God and they agreed to honor the words and agreed to be obedient to them. Then Moses took the blood and sprinkled it on the people and he said, *"Behold the blood of the covenant, which the Lord hath made with you concerning all these words"* (Exodus 24:8b).

The people then responded in joy and once the sacrificial meal was prepared they ate that blessed meal. In truth this was their very first family celebration. They rejoiced over their marriage supper, and they held a public display in full acceptance of their marriage to God. According to Alfred

Edersheim, *Bible History Old Testament*, "And now the covenant was to be inaugurated by sacrifice, the sprinkling of blood, and the sacrificial meal. This transaction was the most important in the whole history of Israel. By this one sacrifice, never renewed, Israel was formally set apart as the people of God; and it lay at the foundation of all the sacrificial worship which followed. Then God instituted the Tabernacle, the priesthood, and all of its services. Thus this one sacrifice prefigured the one sacrifice of our Lord Jesus Christ for His Church." Amen!

To join with God in this great celebration Moses, in obedience, took Aaron and his sons, Nadab and Abihu, and seventy of the elders of Israel up to see their God. In my opinion this is one of the most exciting verses in scripture, for it gives but a small glimpse foretelling the beauty of heaven during the upcoming Marriage Supper of the Lamb in all His glory. *"And they saw the God of Israel: and there was under his feet as it were a paved work of a sapphire stone, and as it were the body of heaven in his clearness. And upon the nobles of the children of Israel he laid not his hand: also they saw God, and did eat and drink" (Exodus 24:10-11).*

Wow, what a moment for the faithful children of God who had now become His bride! They had suffered much, believed much, obeyed their God, and they were in His presence. I thrill over that statement because the day will come when we will stand in His presence and be able to worship Him face to face.

Some may quickly jump on this scripture to remind us of God's own words saying, *"And he said, Thou canst not see my face: for there shall no man see me and live" (Exodus 33:20).* But let me share other scriptures to clarify this apparent contradiction, Moses had asked, *"I beseech thee, shew me thy glory."* And God had responded, *"I will make all my goodness pass before thee, and I will proclaim the name of the Lord before thee; and will be gracious to* whom I will be gracious, and will shew mercy on whom I will shew mercy" (Exodus 33:18-19).

Notice Moses had asked to see God's glory, and recall that God covered Moses with His hand as He went by so that Moses could not see His face but only His back. Also it is recorded, *"(Now the man Moses was very meek, above all the men which were upon the face of the earth)" (Numbers 12:3).*

Also in Numbers 12:6-8, *"And he said, Hear now my words: If there be a prophet among you, I the LORD will make myself known unto him in a vision, and will speak into him in a dream. My servant Moses is not so, who is faithful in all mine house. With him will I speak mouth to mouth, even apparently, and not in dark speeches; and the similitude of the LORD shall he behold: wherefore then were ye not afraid to speak against my servant Moses?"*

Similitude is a form, likeness or image. Another interesting note is that though the scripture said that Moses, Aaron and his sons and the seventy elders saw God, they could not nor did not describe Him. They spoke only of the sapphire pavement under His feet. How can people describe a spirit? We must remember that God had invited the leaders of Israel to meet with Him. It is hard to imagine that God would call them into harm without offering them some sort of protection. I would imagine that God honored them with His *grace and mercy* which served as their protection as noted in Exodus 33:9.

There are more scriptures to consider here. Jesus, at the Sermon on the Mount taught that *"Blessed are the pure in heart: for they shall see God" (Matthew 5:8).* Scripture does say that no man has seen God, John 1:4-12. However, please consider that Adam and Eve saw God, Genesis 3:8. Abraham saw God, Genesis 12:1-8; 13:14-18. Jacob saw God, Genesis 28:13-15 and as is written, Moses often saw God. Wonder of wonders they also ate with Him. Men cannot easily eat if fearful so God must have given them peace. And think of the food, truly out-of-this-world gourmet kosher. Trust me, no shrimp diablo nor baked ham was served at that meal. From the beginning, He went through some tough times in the pursuit of His bride, and through them all, God never wavered. He wanted Israel to be His wife and she was. He was a very happy husband as He entertained Moses, Aaron, his sons, and the elders of Israel. He had high hopes, though being God He knew the outcome that through the years Israel would fight Him all the way.

An Overview of God's Appointed Times and Holy Convocations

*Y*ear after year God's calendar moves on. He has set in place feasts, commemorations, and high holy days. He has set times for fasting and times for joy. His yearly calendar truly proves the goodness of His nature and His plan for all mankind. From the Passover to Booths, God tells the Hebrew story, year after year.

The feasts of God are described as being similar to a rainbow; there are three major feasts: Passover, Pentecost and Tabernacles and four minor ones: Unleavened Bread, Early First Fruits, Trumpets and Atonement. For the Jew, attendance is mandatory at the three major feasts in Jerusalem.

Is it any wonder that we need to study these things since we are Christians? We will do these things and we will celebrate these times, when we begin our eternal life in Heaven. I would like to remind everyone that Jesus already fulfilled the appointed spring times and we wait for His return to complete the fall convocations.

Lord God, I praise You and thank You that there will always be the appointed times in heaven and we will celebrate them with You. We ask to be well taught so that we will rightly show ourselves approved before you. Amen.

Let us recall that it is said, *"Let no man therefore judge you in meat, or in drink, or in respect for an holyday, or of the new moon, or of the sabbath days: Which are a shadow of things to come; but the body is of Christ"* (Colossians 2:16-17). And so, all of these wonderful times, commemorations, and seasons that God has given to the Hebrew people are to be practiced in Heaven and we, the body, will participate in them with joy.

Let us also keep in mind, that before its destruction, most of these festivals and high holy days were celebrated in the Temple. The Temple was the center of daily life for Israel but because of its destruction these festivals were celebrated on a much smaller scale. I will attempt to describe both the old Temple celebrations and the smaller celebrations in the Synagogue and those in the home.

We will study all of these celebrations but let us first look at the order of things. Let us begin by looking at God's perfect calendar. At the beginning of the Jewish year and the arrival of spring, we have the first of God's festivals. It is the Pesach, the Lord's Passover, which most of us remember as the awesome night that God redeemed His bride from Egypt. Quickly following is the feast of Hag Ha Matzah, which we call the Feast of Unleavened Bread, this feast is often overlooked because it is such an intrinsic part of the Passover. Next comes Sfirat Haomer of Early First Fruits, which also becomes the closing day of Passover. On that day of Early First Fruits there begins a counting of days and on the fiftieth day from Early First Fruits we arrive at Shavuot, or the Feast of Weeks, which we know as Pentecost.

There are no special God-appointed times during the summer months which are usually considered the long hot summer and often called the *church age*. For the Jews, however, the month of Av is considered one of the saddest times of their calendar year. In August the Jews experienced the destruction of their fine Temples. It is amazing to see that both Temples, Solomon's Temple and the Second Temple, were destroyed on the same date, the ninth of Av. These horrific events, though years apart, happened on the same day in the month of July/August. Many other dreadful events against the Jews occurred on that day so they call the ninth of Av the saddest day of the year. They named this day Tisha B'Av. It is a time of grieving, fasting and self-denial. Often on this day the Ark of the Synagogue Torah is found draped in black.

As time moves the days of fall are again upon us and we begin God's calendar again. First is Rosh HaShanah, which we call the Feast of Trumpets. That is quickly followed by Yom Kippur, called the Day of Atonement. It is noted that there are ten days between these two most important holy days. These days are called the Ten Days of Awe and we will look at them again since these are very important days for us as Christians. The final festive time on God's calendar is Sukkot, or Booths, which we call the Feast of Tabernacles. God calls Passover, Pentecost, and Tabernacles mandatory times, which means that they must celebrate them in Israel and every year pious Jews from all over the world make every effort in order to celebrate there.

These are the last of the festivals and holy convocations that were called for by God. We know about Hanukkah, which the Jews celebrate because God did a great miracle for them. Let me provide some additional background. Upon the death of Alexander the Great who controlled all the known world at that time, the area known as Judea fell to one of his generals who was named Antiochus. He was an evil man and he and his troops closed the Temple to all Jews. He outlawed all Jewish traditions such as Shabbat, Kosher food laws, and circumcision. They defiled the Temple by erecting statues to the Greek god Zeus and the worst thing he did was to sacrifice a foul pig on the great altar of God. When the Jews reclaimed the Temple, there was only a single day's supply of oil found and it took a full eight days to manufacture the special holy oil for the great Temple lamp. God did a miracle. He made that single cruse of oil burn miraculously in the Temple Menorah for eight days while they worked at fever pitch to make the new consecrated oil. When they saw what God had done they celebrated and continue celebrating even today for that great miracle from God.

Undoubtedly, we have also heard about Purim (PUR-eem) or the Feast of Lots, which is written about in the book of Esther. These are wonderful times, however, we will not study them here since they were not listed in the celebrations that were originally given by God. In this book we will only read about the days that God called appointments because these are the days that make a wonderful road map for us. By learning about these festivals we will soon be able to see a picture of God's great plan for those of us who are Christians. Some of these festivals have been fulfilled and some await completion. Jesus has already fulfilled all the spring festivals and we await Him now to complete His work ahead. The future for the church, the Bride of Christ, is clearly detailed in those coming plans and it should be a most exciting time.

Please understand that this information is as I have learned it. There are some things that have been deliberately omitted that are not pertinent to the stories as they affect the Christians who are reading this book.

Shabbat, the Sabbath

*O*nce we are in Heaven we will keep that special time. God created the world and everything in and around it and He then rested on the seventh day. So He asked His children to join in His rest on the seventh day. This was to be a family day, a day of rest from the outside world where a man could take time to enjoy life within the bosom of his family. It was to be a day when everyone reflected upon God and joy in Him would fill the house.

Children were free to ask questions about God and the father would teach them. It was to be a day of love and gentleness with extended family and the immediate family all reflecting about the wonders of their God.

"Moreover also I gave then my sabbaths, to be a sign between me and them, that they might know that I am the Lord that sanctify them" (Ezekiel 20:12).

God intended that the Sabbath be a day of joy and delight, but over the years the rabbis added rules and restrictions, therefore the day became less than God had intended. If we recall, Jesus Himself struggled with some of the regulations that had been put upon the people which were not originally intended by God. Every time He healed someone on the Sabbath there would be accusations. Read Matthew 12:5, Luke 6:1-5, Luke 6:6-12, and John 5:19. It is also important to note that, *"...The Sabbath was made for man, and not man for the Sabbath: Therefore the Son of man is Lord of the sabbath"* (Mark 2:27-28).

It was once recorded that the Jews worshiped on the Shabbat not because it was so common, but that it was so special they observed it every seven days. Preparation for the Shabbat began early on Friday because there are certain work restrictions and all the cooking had to be completed before the Shabbat began. For example, the turning on of stoves was not allowed once the Shabbat began. Since all the days were marked from sunset to sunset, then the Shabbat would begin when three stars were seen in the sky or eighteen minutes before sunset on Friday evening, which is the Eve of Shabbat. Since the food was already prepared and the best linens draped the table, the very best china was in place, and two candlesticks were prominently displayed. While looking upon them the Jews were reminded of their sanctification.

The most important time of that Shabbat evening meal is when the woman dons her headscarf and lights the candles. She circles her fingers over the light from the candle and draws the warmth of the candles to cover her eyes. She then repeats the blessing, "Blessed art Thou, Lord our God, King of the Universe, who has set us apart by Your commandments and has commanded us to kindle the Sabbath lights." A blessing is said over the wine and the challah, which is the bread. The bread is covered during the blessings spoken over the wine since tradition records that the challah would not be insulted when the wine is blessed first. Then a very special blessing is spoken when the father puts his hand on the head of his son and says, "May God make you like Ephraim and Manasseh." If there is a daughter then the father will bless her with, "May you be like Sarah, Rebekah and Leah." There is also a blessing for the wife that comes from Proverbs 31:10-31. The well-prepared meal is enjoyed leisurely with family and friends. The grace is said after dinner because no one would thank God for a meal which they had not yet tasted. If there is a Shabbat eve service at the synagogue then the family goes to worship their God happily and with a proper and good attitude.

The first sounds a person would hear upon waking on Saturday morning would be *Shabbat Shalom*, a greeting much like a prayer, asking for it to be a peaceful Sabbath. Shalom is a word with which we are familiar, however we usually do not have complete understanding. Shalom comes from the word Shalem, which means nothing missing and nothing broken. It really demonstrates the complete fullness in God.

Preparations are made to attend the regular synagogue services, which follow the same basic pattern since the times of Ezra and Nehemiah. Some Psalms are sung, there are readings and chantings from the Torah, and a proper preaching of the message. After the final hymn the service comes to a close with a little wine and refreshments, a moment which is called the *Delight of the Shabbat*. This little delight comes from the words of the Prophet Isaiah, *"If thou turn away thy foot from the sabbath, from doing thy pleasure on my holy day; and call the sabbath a delight, the holy of the* Lord, *honorable; and shalt honour him, not doing thine own ways, nor finding thine own pleasure, nor speaking thine own words: Then shalt thou delight thyself in the* Lord; *and I will cause thee to ride upon the high places of the earth, and feed thee with the heritage of Jacob thy father: for the mouth of the Lord hath spoken it"* (Isaiah 58:13-14).

The rest of the day is spent eating previously prepared foods and leisurely savoring the memories and recollections of their day with God, but as the day comes to a close there will be one more special moment. It is called the Havdalah, which means *separated*, since God has separated the Jewish people from the world, unto Himself. This is an at-home family moment and begins by the setting out of a specially-braided candle with at least two wicks, a spice box filled with cloves and cinnamon, and a wine cup sitting on a saucer. Then the father reads, *"Behold, God is my salvation; I will trust, and not be afraid: for the* Lord Jehovah *is my strength and my song; he also is become my salvation. Therefore with joy shall ye draw water out of the wells of salvation"* (Isaiah 12:2-3). Songs are sung, scriptures are quoted, the cup is poured and the blessing over the wine is spoken, which is the same blessing used from the night before.

It is interesting to note that the wine cup is first placed in a saucer and then the cup is filled. It is filled to overflowing because their God is an overwhelming God and their lives in Him overflow with goodness. Then the cup and saucer is passed around and everyone takes a sip. Next the spice box is blessed. The father holds the box in his right hand and says, "Blessed are you, Lord our God, King of the Universe, Creator of the fruit of various kinds of spices." The spice box is then passed for everyone to shake and then to sniff.

Then the father lights the candle, he lights it and holds it upright over the wine filled saucer and says, "Blessed are you Lord our God, King of the Universe, Creator over the lights of fire." It is traditional for a person to hold fingers in a partial fist near the flame of the candle with the nails facing up. This allows the light to shine through the fingernails and casts a shadow in the palm, showing the separation of night from day. Following is a series of prayers until the last song is sung.

The final blessing is spoken and then the candle is extinguished by dipping it in the saucer of wine. Then as the celebrants greeted each other with, "Shabbat Shalom" at the beginning of the Shabbat they would say, "Shavu'ah Tov," which means to have a good week. Because they obey God and spend this time together with Him they become revived and well-able to face their regular weekly duties which lie ahead.

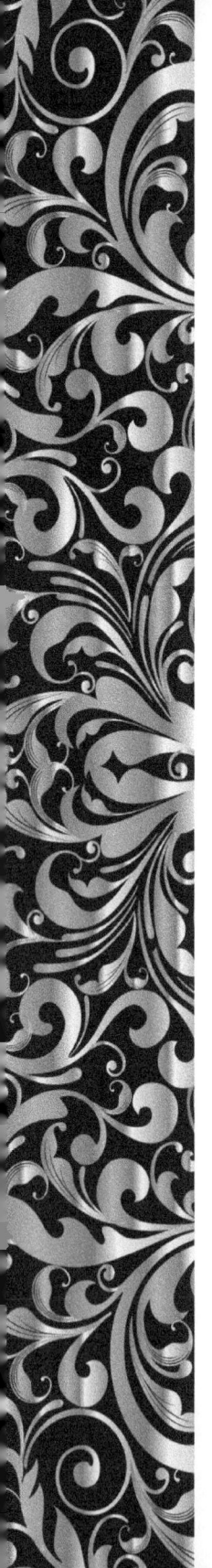

God's Appointed Times, Fulfilled

Pesach, The Feast of Passover

A HOLY CONVOCATION ALSO CALLED JUMP OVER; THE FIRST APPOINTED TIME OF GOD. IT WAS FULFILLED WHEN JESUS OFFERED HIMSELF AS THE SACRIFICIAL LAMB.

"In the fourteenth day of the first month at even is the LORD's passover. And on the fifteenth day of the same month is the feast of unleavened bread unto the LORD: seven days ye must eat unleavened bread. In the first day ye shall have an holy convocation: and ye shall do no servile work therein. But ye shall offer an offering made by fire unto the LORD seven days: in the seventh day is a holy convocation: ye shall do no servile work therein" (Leviticus 23:5-8).

This celebration is the oldest continuously celebrated religious festival in the world. The story is found in the books of Genesis and Exodus, and it is a yearly celebration which lasts eight days. It stands as a reminder of the seasons of the Hebrew people who were exiled in Egypt and for the Jews it was the true sign of spring.

God brought Israel, the patriarch and father of the twelve Hebrew tribes, into the land of Egypt, *"And he said, I am God, the God of thy father: fear not to go down to Egypt; for I will there make of thee a great nation: I will go down with thee into Egypt; and I will surely bring thee up again:" (Genesis 46:3-4a).*

The time of Israel's sojourn, and the time of the Hebrew people in Egypt was a remarkable 430 years. Though sometimes we wonder if God has lost

or forgotten us, He never will. For the Hebrew people God became only a name, a name to wonder about. But as He had made a promise to Israel, He remembered when the time was right and perfect. We must never lose heart because God will always keep His promise.

In previous chapters I shared the *Introduction to the Hebrew People* and the background history of how they came into Egypt. In this history of the Holy Convocations I am writing here just a general overview. My hope is that every reader will hunger for a deeper study. Many books are readily available, so I pray that each reader will seek more information. Also I shared the marvelous plans of God with the timely arrival of Moses and Aaron to encourage the Hebrew people. God had not forsaken them and was true to His promise to their patriarchs. Once they agreed with God's battle plan then Moses and Aaron began the mighty struggle for their freedom, which was marvelously waged by God against Pharaoh.

Let's recall the challenge before Pharaoh when Moses cast down his rod and it became a snake and that snake handily devoured the snakes of all the magicians of the Egyptians. Then came the ten plagues, the blood, the frogs and the lice, the stinging flies, the murrain and the boils, then the hail, the locusts, the darkness, and then finally the smiting of the first born. All of these were by the plan of God for the redemption of His people. Moses was his Groomsman and He wanted His bride freed and marriage was on His mind.

Since that last night in Egypt the Jewish people have marked this time in celebration of their great victory, which was wrought by the great hand of God. The Jews call it the Pesach and some call it the Jump Over since the death angel did jump over the homes marked with blood. We call it Passover.

During the days when the Temple was in use every Jew who was the head of a household traveled to the Temple to buy a spotless lamb on the 10th day of the Month of Nissan, which we call March/April. The lamb was safely held until the 14th of the month when fathers and sons took the lamb to the Temple in preparation for the sacrificial slaying. The Priest, dressed in scarlet robes, carefully examined the lamb and then watched the father and son as they laid their hands upon the innocent lamb, publicly recognizing before God that the lamb would be taking their place as the sacrifice. The father took the knife and slayed the lamb as the priest caught the blood in gold and silver basins. Then the priest poured the blood upon the altar and the Levites sang the great Hallel (Psalm 111-113). This scene continued over and over and over again, until the close of the totally awesome day.

It is interesting to note that each and every sacrificial lamb purchased at the Temple came from the fields of Bethlehem, which God correctly used as the birthplace of Jesus. Those fields were owned and controlled by the wealthy families of the High Priests. It was a very profitable business! It is also interesting to note that when Jesus came into Jerusalem it was in the midst of the day of the sacrificial slaying. The multitude saw and recognized Him, and spread their garments before Him while they sang, *Hosanna to the Son of David: Blessed is He that cometh in the Name of the Lord; Hosanna in the highest.* That scripture comes from Psalm 118:25-26 and Matthew 21:9, and is this not amazing? These were the very same songs that the Levites had been singing. These songs were sung at the Temple during the sacrifice of each innocent lamb. Those who heard the crowds cry out were some of the foreign travelers who had come to celebrate the Passover. They questioned who this man was who caused the people to spread their garments before him. Those who were praising Him were many of the fathers and their sons who were taking their lambs to be slaughtered and Jesus was in their midst.

The Present Day Preparation of the Seder, the Meal of Order

In preparation for the family Seder, one of the very first duties of every Jewish housewife is the total cleansing of her home. She scours each room, every corner, and all the floors. She cleans the walls and the ceiling, and she totally scours every single cabinet. Nothing will be left untouched and her preparations will be legendary. She packs away all the equipment that is used on a regular basis throughout the year. All the glassware, dishware, pots and pans and every cooking utensil is carefully stowed away until after the Seder.

Once that is completed then all of the Seder equipment is brought out of storage, all of the kitchen equipment, every pot and pan. All baking utensils and all of the usable cooking equipment is brought into the kitchen and carefully washed and put away in the newly-cleaned cabinets. All fine glassware, china, silverware, trays and all special silver implements that are used in preparation of the fine Seder meal must be spotless.

The question is asked, why is all this work and effort necessary? The answer is easy, leaven represented sin! That dreaded leaven must not be found in her house.

If perchance the children had taken a sandwich to their rooms and, God forbid, all the crumbs had not been returned to the kitchen, then the mother searches until she finds every drop of leaven. All of this was for a purpose, God had spoken it, *"Seven days shall ye eat unleavened bread; even the first day ye shall put away leaven out of your houses: for whosoever eateth leavened bread from the first day until the seventh day, that soul shall be cut off from Israel" (Exodus 12:15).*

It is interesting to notice that when Jesus came into the Temple on that day, *"And they came into Jerusalem: and Jesus went into the temple, and began to cast out them that sold and bought in the temple, and overthrew the tables of the moneychangers, and the seats of them that sold doves; And would not suffer that any man should carry any vessel through the temple. And he taught, saying unto them, Is it not written, My house shall be called of all nations the house of prayer? but ye have made it a den of thieves" (Mark 11:15-17).*

It has always pleased me that Jesus was not shy about doing women's work. He struck down those who did evil in His Father's house and just as every good Jewish housewife did that day, He cleansed His Father's house from leaven.

At the end of the day and the night before Passover when the father is home from his work place, he teaches his children about the evils of leaven. The children have been watching their mother as she prepared their house for Passover and it is the job of the father to search the house for leaven. The children follow him as he walks through the house carrying a candle, a large wooden spoon and a feather. He uses the candle to check out each bedroom and then announces that there is no leaven. He moves into the more public rooms and finds no leaven. The children are thrilled as their father declares that so far he has found no leaven. Finally he enters the kitchen. He and his wife previously collaborate so she hides away a small cookie crumb in an otherwise spotlessly clean cabinet. It is the final place that the father will inspect. The children are thrilled with their mother since she kept a totally unleavened home. The final cabinet door is opened and they stand aghast, their father deftly uses the candle and finds leaven in their cabinet. Then the father shows them how to carefully remove the leaven by brushing it with the feather and carefully dispatching it into the large wooden spoon. Once this is complete then the father takes the candle, and the large wooden spoon containing the leaven, and followed by the children, he walks outside the walls of their home. He carefully dispatches the leaven, burning it with the fire from the candle. After his explanation about the search for leaven he declares, "Let any leaven within this home which has been hidden from me, be considered as null and void like the dust of the earth." His job is done, his children have been taught, and he can return to his home to rejoice in a secure Passover season.

It is easier for us to appreciate scriptures when we have a broader understanding of Jewish traditions. Recall with me, *"Then led they Jesus from Caiaphas unto the hall of judgment: and it was early; and they themselves went not into the judgment hall, lest they should be defiled; but they might eat the passover. Pilate then went out unto them, and said, What accusation bring ye against this man?" (John 18:28-29).* These Jewish rabbis understood only too clearly that the court of the Roman leader would not be as a cleansed Jewish home.

They wanted Jesus dispatched without any liability, so they answered Pilate's charge, *"Take ye him, and judge him according to your law. The Jews therefore said unto him, It is not lawful for us to put any man to death:" (John 18:31).* What a travesty! They wanted Jesus killed and removed from the walls of Jerusalem to keep their city cleansed, so they would have no personal responsibility or accountability. It is amazing that today the thought the leaven of this immoral act with the death of Jesus would not deter them from enjoying and eating their Passover celebration.

There are moments when I read certain scriptures that cause me to shudder as I imagine what the outcome will be at that final Day of Judgment. Only God really knows the mental and spiritual condition of any of the High Priests from the Temple. He also knows if any of them ever wondered for a moment if Jesus was indeed the Son of the living God.

The Seder Meal

When the dining room is set, the table is well-covered with the very best linens, and the finest stemware and china is put in place. Now is the time for the last details.

First will be the filling of the matzah plate which is to be covered by a decorated cloth. Then three full sheets of matzah are installed in the Matzah Tosh, which is a beautifully decorated fabric container that will hold the matzah. Each sheet is separated from the other by a linen cloth carefully sewn into the Tosh. To the Jews these represent Abraham, Isaac and Jacob. Those of us who know the truth soon realize that these separated matzah sheets really represent the Father, the Son and the Holy Spirit. They will also need a fine linen cloth about the size of a man's handkerchief.

Next there will be the wine, or a nonalcoholic grape juice, with goblets called Kiddush cups, enough for each guest to enjoy the traditional four sips of wine. There will also be a very special table setting and a cup reserved for Elijah. There will be a beautiful pitcher filled with wine for refilling the cups when needed.

Finally there is a special pitcher, basin and towel, for the ceremonial washing and drying of the hands. And each place setting has a clearly written copy of the *Agam Haggadah*, which is read in order to direct the service and make proper explanation for everyone.

The table is set with a beautifully decorated Seder plate, which holds a series of small cups that is filled with the traditional food stuffs of the Passover celebration. One of the cups will hold bitter greens, which represent the Karpas. There will be a bowl of vinegar or salted water representing the tears of the early Hebrews. One of the small cups will hold extremely hot horseradish representing the bitter herbs called the Maror. A special mixture of chopped apples and ground nuts called Haroset is put on the table which represents the mortar used by the early Jews to set the bricks in place at the building sites of the Egyptians. There will also be an unbroken roasted shank bone of a lamb. At a later date the rabbis added a hard cooked egg, which represented life.

Before the meal begins there are certain scriptures and blessings that are spoken by the host. The meal then begins in the traditional way as the wife covers her head and lights the candles and says, "Blessed are you Lord our God, King of the Universe, Who has set us apart by His Commandments and commanded us to kindle the Passover lights."

The meal begins with the pouring of the first cup. There will be a total of five cups. Four cups will be poured for the guests at the table and the fifth will be set at the place reserved for Elijah. The four cups come from a response by God to the appeals made by the Hebrew people. The first cup represents that God heard His people and the cup is called the Cup of Sanctification. The second represents God's Covenant, and is called the Cup of Judgment. It is also called by some the Cup of Plagues, Praise or Woes. The third cup represents that God looked upon them and it is called the Cup of Redemption. Later we will see that this is the cup that Jesus chose to designate the beginning of the Lord's Supper. The fourth and last cup represents that God has respect for them and the cup is called the Cup of Acceptance. These four cups are born from the "I wills," spoken by God, *"Wherefore say unto the children of Israel, I am the LORD, and I will bring you out from under the burdens of the Egyptians, and I will rid you out of their bondage, and I will redeem you with a stretched out arm, and with great judgments: And I will take you to me for a people, and I will be to you a God: and ye shall know that I am the* LORD *your God, which bringeth you out from under the burdens of the Egyptians" (Exodus 6:6-7).*

The blessing is said over the first cup, "Be blessed, God, our God, King of the Universe, Who chose us out of all the peoples, exalted us above all tongues, and sanctified us by His commandments. And lovingly, You gave us, God, our God, set times for celebration, festivals and occasions for rejoicing, this Matzah festival, and this holiday, this holy convocation, the occasion of our liberation, a holy convocation in remembrance of the Exodus from Egypt. Indeed, You chose us and sanctified us from among all the people, and Your holy set times, happily and joyously did You bequeath to us. Be blessed, God, Who sanctified Israel and the festivals." The first cup is consumed and now all are sanctified.

Then begins the reading of the Haggadah with the declaration, "Yesterday we were slaves, today we are free. In urgent haste we departed from Egypt." The Seder matzah tray is lifted and the poverty bread is blessed.

The host then takes the water and washes his hands. In a like moment when Jesus took the water and began to wash the feet of the disciples; even the feet of Judas received His ministration. The Lord took advantage of this opportunity to stop the bickering among these men, concerning who would be the greatest in His kingdom. *"So after he had washed their feet, and had taken his garments, and was set down again, he said unto them, Know ye what I have done to you? Ye call me Master and Lord: and ye say well; for so I am. If I then, your Lord and Master, have washed your feet; ye also ought to wash one another's feet. For I have given you an example, that ye should do as I have done to you. Verily, verily, I say unto you, The servant is not greater than his lord; neither he that is sent greater than he that sent him. If ye know these things, happy are ye if ye do them"* (John 13:12-17). The Evangelical Dictionary of Theology states, "The complete bath represents salvation, symbolized by baptism. The washing of the feet symbolizes the need that believers have for repeated cleansing from contact with the sinful world."

Next in the Seder meal we eat of the Karpas, the bitter greens, which are dipped into the salted water. The blessing states, "Blessed are You O Lord our God, King of the Universe who created the fruit of the earth." The bitterness of the greens and the salted water reminds the Jews of the bitter time in Egypt and the salted water is reminiscent of their many tears.

The following step is extremely important to the Jews and to those of us who believe. It is the time to prepare the Afikoman (Afee-komen) which in Greek means, *the Last*. This preparation is conducted in front of the guests. The host carefully removes the centerpiece of matzah from the Matzah Tosh, and breaks it into two pieces; those pieces will be laid together and carefully wrapped and folded in a linen cloth about the size of a man's handkerchief. The children are then instructed to cover their eyes while the piece of broken matzah is hidden away out of everybody's sight until the last part of the meal.

Now the host lifts and uncovers the matzah tray and then he says, "We were Pharaoh's slaves in Egypt. And God, our God, took us out of there with a strong hand and outstretched arm. If the Blessed Holy One had not taken our ancestors out of Egypt, we, our children, and our children's children would still be enslaved to Pharaoh in Egypt. And even if all of us were wise, even if all of us were clever, even if all of us were sages, even if all of us knew the Torah—we would still be in duty bound to talk about the Exodus from Egypt. The more we elaborate on the story of the Exodus from Egypt, the more praiseworthy we become."

The second cup of wine is poured and then the children participate by asking four questions:

1) Why, on all other nights, do we eat either leavened bread or matzah, but tonight we eat only matzah?

2) Why, on all other nights, do we eat all kinds of vegetables, but tonight we make a special point of eating bitter herbs?

3) Why, on all other nights, do we not make a point of dipping at all, but tonight we make a point of dipping twice?

4) Why, on all other nights, do we eat either sitting up or reclining, but tonight we all make a point of reclining?

Then the Jews recognize the bread of affliction. "This is the bread which our ancestors ate in the Land of Egypt. Then we were slaves; now we are free!" But for those of us who are Christians we know that the sinless bread is our beloved Lord Jesus. It is good to be reminded that He was the bread of life and as the host lifts a piece of the poverty bread we remember that; *"Surely he hath borne our griefs, and carried our sorrows: yet we did esteem him stricken, smitten of God, and afflicted. But he was wounded for our transgressions, he was bruised for our iniquities: the chastisement of our peace was upon him; and with his stripes we are healed. All we like sheep have gone astray; we have turned every one to his own way; and the L*ORD *hath laid on him the iniquity of us all"* (Isaiah 53:4-6).

A narrative is usually read here concerning the four sons in the mind of the Torah... the wise son, the wicked son, the simple son, and the son who does not know how to ask. However this is often skipped over for the sake of brevity.

Now we come to the drama of the Passover meal, the plagues. The narration begins with the reminiscing of their trip to Egypt. They begin, "Originally, our ancestors were idolators, but now the Omnipresent has drawn us to His service, as said in

Joshua 23:2-4: Joshua then said to the entire people: this is the word of God the God of Israel: Long ago your ancestors lived beyond the river, (Euphrates) – Terah, Abraham's father and Nahor's father – and they worshiped other gods. But I took your father Abraham from beyond the river and led him through the whole Land of Canaan, and I gave him many descendants: I gave him Isaac, and to Isaac I gave Jacob and Esau. Then I gave Esau the hill country of Seir to possess, while Jacob and his children went down to Egypt."

"Blessed be the One who keeps His promise to Israel, Blessed be He. For the Blessed Holy One predestined the end of the Egyptian bondage, doing what He told Our Father Abraham in the Covenant between the Sections, as said: *'And he said to Abram, Know for certain that your descendants will be strangers in a land not theirs, and they, (the host people) will enslave and oppress them (the Jews) for 400 years. But I will also judge the nation they will serve, and in the end they will leave with great wealth'" (Genesis 15:13-14)*. Most of this is found in the Jewish *Agam Haggadah*.

There is a reading of each plague, and when the name of each one is solemnly called out, then those who are in attendance will either spill a small drop of wine, or dip their finger into the wine and drop it on the small plate that has been offered. With each drop the body bemoans the hard times that the Jews had in Egypt. These are the ten plagues which the Blessed Holy One brought on the Egyptians in Egypt: blood, frogs, lice, wild beasts, which were the stinging flies, murrain, boils, hail, locusts, darkness, and the smiting of the firstborn.

With the completion of the calling out of the ten plagues the Host carefully passes among his guests and offer water and a towel for the washing and drying of their hands. At this time he will say, "Be blessed, God our God, King of the Universe, who has sanctified us by His Commandments and commanded us concerning the rinsing of the hands."

The host then breaks a piece of matzah and passes the matzah around so that each one may break a piece for his or her own use. The host reminds his guests that in the Temple this was called the Passover sacrifice to God, because He passed over the houses of the Hebrew people when He smote the Egyptians, then in those days the people would bow down and prostrate themselves. The host then points to the matzah and reminds everyone that the bread was unleavened because there was no time to leaven the bread; they left Egypt in a hurry. Now the time comes to break some of the matzah in order to taste. The host points to the bitter herb and remind his guests that they eat the bitter herb because their lives were embittered by the hard labor of brick making, and all other kinds of ruthless work. Now is the time to apply a small piece of the bitter herb to a small piece of the matzah for a taste.

Please be very careful because most people use very hot horseradish for the bitter herb. We need to remember that we are to suffer along with the Jewish people.

Once everyone is able to function again then they may make a small sandwich called the Koresh, choosing to add a small sliver of lamb to a piece of matzah, adding a small spoon full of the Haroset, the chopped apples and nut mixture, and then adding some more horseradish. Some will dip it in the vinegar before they eat. This is a very special mix because this is considered to be like the piece that Jesus fed to Judas. *"When Jesus had thus said, he was troubled in spirit, and testified, and said, Verily, verily, I say unto you, that one of you shall betray me. Then the disciples looked one on another, doubting of whom he spake. Now there was leaning on Jesus' bosom one of his disciples, whom Jesus loved. Simon Peter therefore beckoned to him, that he should ask who it should be of whom he spake. He then lying on Jesus' breast saith unto him, Lord, who is it? Jesus answered, He it is, to whom I shall give a sop, when I have dipped it. And when he had dipped the sop, he gave it to Judas Iscariot, the son of Simon. And after the sop Satan entered into him. Then said Jesus unto him, That thou doest, do quickly. Now no man at the table knew for what intent he spake this unto him. For some of them thought, because Judas had the bag, that Jesus had said unto him, Buy those things that we have need of against the feast; or, that he should give something to the poor. He then having received the sop went immediately out: and it was night (John 13:21-30).*

The table becomes cleared as the traditional Passover meal is almost finished. Now will come a full-scale and wonderful dinner. The feast includes soup, roast beef or lamb, multiple vegetables, potatoes, assortments of salads and matzah. The table is filled with wonderful food and everyone enjoys the fabulous meal. The dishes are cleared off the table again and the dessert is then served. Everything that has been served has been wonderfully made without flour. Even the delicious chocolate cake is flourless.

The children are quick to remind the host that the celebration is not yet finished. There is one more special moment to enjoy. Of course, they are talking about the Afikomen, which is the ransom of the hidden matzah. Remember, at the beginning of the meal the host broke matzah and wrapped it in white linen and then carefully hid the special package away in a nearby room. Children never forget this part of the meal since there is a financial reward awaiting the one who finds the hidden package.

Remember that these were Jewish children who would not know about the story of the ransom of Jesus by Judas and the high priests, so they would not be affected by its horror. Let's recall the scripture, *"Then one of the twelve, called Judas Iscariot, went unto the chief priests, And said unto them, What will ye give* me, and I will deliver him unto you? And they covenanted with him for thirty pieces of silver. And from that time he saw opportunity to betray him" (Matthew 26:14-16).

As we come back to the dinner table we find the host has arranged for the elder children to allow the youngest to find the folded package that had been hidden away. The parents encourage the search by shouting, *You are too cold! Look the other way! Now you are getting warmer!* Finally the youngster finds the revered package and carefully returns the package to the host. Payment is made and the child is overjoyed. Then the host carefully unwraps the final piece and breaks the bread so that each guest can have one piece of the special matzah, and then he carefully fills the third cup. The third cup is the Cup of Redemption.

These are the pieces, the elements that Jesus used to create and serve the First Communion. As it is written, they were eating and Jesus took the bread and blessed it. He said, "Blessed are you Lord our God, King of the Universe, Who brings forth bread from the earth." He then broke it and gave it to His disciples and said, *"Take, eat; this is my body. And he took the cup, and gave thanks, and gave it to them, saying, Drink ye all of it; For this is my blood of the new testament, which is shed for many for the remission of sins. But I say unto you, I will not drink henceforth of this fruit of the vine, until that day when I drink it new with you in my Father's kingdom. And when they had sung an hymn, they went out into the Mount of Olives"* (Matthew 26:26b-30).

When Jesus says that He will drink the cup of the wine with us in His Father's Kingdom, could He be alluding to the Bridal Cup? I don't know, but it is a wonderful thought.

As one of the final acts in the meal the host says Grace. They thank God for the food they have eaten. I once asked why they say Grace at the end of the meal instead of the beginning as we do. The answer came in a straightforward manner, *Why would you thank God for a meal that you have not tasted? It might be a bad meal and you wouldn't want to thank God for a bad meal would you?* The meal closes with the singing and recitation of the Psalms. They pray that God accepts their service through the meal. Now the host pours the fourth cup. This is the cup that Jesus did not drink, the Cup of Acceptance. Instead of drinking the Cup of Acceptance He went to Gethsemane, accepted His Father's will and went to the cross for all of us. In the final move the host fills the cup that has been set aside for Elijah. He opens the front door to see if Elijah has come to tell them that the Messiah has arrived. This role was taken by John the Baptist when he pronounced the good news to the Jewish people during the Baptism of Jesus. The host then stands at his front door to pray. This is pretty much the end of the Passover meal except to make the final proclamation, "Next year in Jerusalem."

In every Jewish household this meal is conducted and enjoyed pretty much as I have described it here. Each year at Passover, the family gathers and repeats this historic plan. I ask that every reader pray for the Jews, those known and those not yet known. Pray that they will come to understand the true fullness of this meal that the Father has designed, and that they may accept that the Messiah has come indeed and His name is Jesus.

Anyone who has a growing interest in the Passover can purchase a copy of the *Agam Haggadah* at most bookstores. They can even be found at most grocery stores during the Passover season.

Hag Ha Matzah, the Feast of Unleavened Bread

This is the second appointed time of God, the second day of Passover which was fulfilled when Jesus was sacrificed and died for us.

"Purge out therefore the old leaven, that ye may be a new lump, as ye are unleavened. For even Christ our passover is sacrificed for us:" (1 Corinthians 5:7).

This feast is often overlooked because it is such an integral part of the Passover and it commences immediately after the Pascal night, the night of the Seder. *"Seven days shall ye eat unleavened bread; even the first day ye shall put away leaven out of your houses: for whosoever eateth leavened bread from the first day unto the seventh day, that soul shall be cut off from Israel"* (Exodus 12:15).

"In the fourteenth day of the first month at even is the Lord's passover. And on the fifteenth day of the same month is the feast of unleavened bread unto the Lord: seven days ye must eat unleavened bread" (Leviticus 23:5-6).

During this seven-day appointed time the only breadstuff allowed in a Jewish house is matzah. It stands as a tangible symbol of the hardships that afflicted the Hebrew children during their years of slavery.

When we recall the original Passover night, the people were driven away in such haste that there was no time for the leavening of their bread. God had already instructed that the chometz, the leaven, was to be destroyed.

It is unfortunate that many Christians seldom use matzah. For those willing to take a moment and hold a piece of matzah up to the light, they would see the blessing of God. The first thing to notice is the piercing, and then the marks of the bruising. God designed this bread as a sinless offering, a picture of His Son. *"But he was wounded for our transgressions, he was bruised for our iniquities: the chastisement of our peace was upon him; and with his stripes we are healed" (Isaiah 53:5).* And when we use matzah in the communion we hold in our hands not just the likeness of Jesus, but a piece of His healing power.

Let me explain. There was a Sunday, not a special one, but it was the time for Communion. Since this was at the Tab, my former church where Jamie presided we had small pieces of unleavened bread serving as the body of our Lord Jesus. The elements had been served and Jamie was explaining the scriptures, but instead of taking the bread and wine, he stepped down and served a newcomer in the church. She was evidently Jewish and the signs of illness were upon her. The God of the Christians was her last hope. She hesitated but Jamie was very gentle and convincing, and so she accepted. As she left the church that day all who were able touched her with love. She returned the following week and she evidenced more strength. Total healing came upon her, visit by visit to the church. Once the total healing was hers she told us that though her God had sent her to the church, it was when she received Jesus through His body and His blood that the healing was manifested. Hallelujah! I find it difficult to stop talking about the goodness of our God Who has already made every preparation we could possibly need in the life we live here on earth, as we live and prepare to join Him in Heaven.

"The Omer," the Time Between Passover and Pentecost

This period called the Omer begins on the second night of Passover and continues until Shavuot, which we call Pentecost.

For the Jew the count recalls the Sinai. It is the remembrance of the location and the time when God gave them the law which is called the Torah. This is a special anniversary for them for the giving of the law separated them from all men. Before this special day men lived as they pleased with no direction to guide them. God had already separated the Jews unto Himself and now He separated the Jews from the rest of mankind.

In the Oxford Universal Dictionary the word Omer is translated as a Hebrew word meaning: a Hebrew dry measure of capacity equal to the tenth part of an ephah. It also means a sheaf, i.e., the sheaf of the wave offering. Scripture has several mentions of the Omer but my favorite is, *"And Moses said unto Aaron, Take a pot, and put an omer full of manna therein, and lay it up before the L*ORD*, to be kept for your generations" (Exodus 16:33).*

This special measure, of the early first grain offering, was to be brought to the Temple on the 16th of Nissan. For the Jew, the Torah commanded that seven weeks be counted from the time of the first offering. *"And the L*ORD *spake unto Moses, saying, Speak unto the children of Israel, and say unto them, When ye be come into the land which I give unto you, and shall reap the harvest thereof, then ye shall bring a sheaf of the firstfruits of your harvest unto the priest: And he shall wave the sheaf before the L*ORD*, to be accepted for you: on the morrow after the sabbath the priest* *shall wave it. (Leviticus 23:9-11).* It is interesting to note that in this scripture God is promising His people the benefits from harvest and as yet they see no fields fit for planting, nor do they have seed to be planted since they are living in the middle of an arid desert. However, God spoke of the future but He keeps all of His promises!

The time of the Omer count leads us to Shavuot. In truth Shavuot does not have a fixed date on the calendar since it falls on the day after the completion of the Omer count, which is the fiftieth day after the Omer counting is brought to the Temple. Though there is currently no Temple they are still commanded to count all the days between Passover and Shavuot.

The question is asked about the importance of counting the days from the bringing of the Omer until Shavuot. The answer is simple. Since this was to be the first spring harvest a thanksgiving to God must be offered, and the offering would come from the very first barley leaves. The Jews have always kept in mind that if they thank God for the early harvest, then He will be faithful to give a latter harvest. For this we Christians must give thanks, for in God's eye we are the latter harvest.

Every participating Jew will receive a booklet with directions for keeping the count. The counting is done at night when the new day begins. The procedure begins by standing and then saying "Praised are You, Lord our God, Ruler of the Universe, Who has sanctified us with His Commandments, commanding us to count the Omer." This is followed by the count for the day: "Today is the first day of the Omer." The weeks are also counted. For example, "Today is the 18th day of the Omer, which equals two weeks and four days of the Omer." During this time it is advised that money be set aside for each day of the count. For the modern day Jew this would stand as an offering, to be given to the poor at the final day of the count.

There are basic rules that must be followed through the time of the Omer count. People may mourn for the dead but they are forbidden to marry. Hair must not be cut, and some men choose not to shave. People may not attend musical concerts. However, tradition has it that they may shoot arrows aimed at devils. Leather shoes are forbidden. This is a common restriction since it brings to mind the golden calf during the wilderness experience. As a positive note, bonfires may be lighted.

The blessing of the counting is the daily remembrance to the coming of Shavuot. Though this time was considered as a counting, it was not as a count down but a count up to the next great festival of God.

Sfirat Haomer, Early First Fruits

This is the third appointed time of God, which sometimes was called Yom HaBikkurim which was fulfilled when Jesus rose from the dead.

"And ye shall offer that day when ye wave the sheaf an he lamb without blemish of the first year for a burnt offering unto the Lord. And the meat offering thereof shall be two tenth deals of fine flour mingled with oil, an offering made by fire unto the Lord for a sweet savour: and the drink offering thereof shall be of wine, the fourth part of an hin. And ye shall eat neither bread, nor parched corn, nor green ears, until the selfsame day that ye have brought an offering unto your God: it shall be a statute for ever throughout your generations in all *your dwellings. And ye shall count unto you from the morrow after the sabbath, from the day that ye brought the sheaf of the wave offering; seven sabbaths shall be complete: Even unto the morrow after the seventh sabbath shall ye number fifty days; and ye shall offer a new meat offering unto the LORD"* (Leviticus 23:12-14).

This is the third day of Passover and it was fulfilled when on that day, our beloved Lord Jesus rose from the dead. *"But now is Christ risen from the dead, and become the firstfruits of them that slept. For since by man came death, by man came also the resurrection of the dead. For as in Adam all die, even so in Christ shall all be made alive. But every man in his own order: Christ the firstfruits; afterward they that are Christ's at his coming"* (1 Corinthians 15:20-23).

It is also pertinent to read:

"Jesus answered and said unto them, Destroy this temple, and in three days I will raise it up" (John 2:19).

Sfirat Haomer is known as *the counting of the sheaf.* It is the earliest Israeli harvest and like the Sukkot in the fall, it emphasizes the agrarian nature of that ancient land. During these days at the Temple there was a rather elaborate ceremony of bringing the offering of thanksgiving tithes to God. A priest would meet a group of Jewish men who were carrying their offerings of their first fruit and he would lead them up to the Temple mount. As they walked along, the priest would lead them in praise to God. There would be shouting, dancing and singing of praises of joy to their beloved God. The priest would take some of the sheaves and lift them in the air and wave them in every direction proving that God is sovereign over all the land and in every direction.

Arguments ensued between the Jewish religious factions as to the correct timing of the festival. The major factors were of course the Pharisees and the Sadducees, but even they were divided. It all had to do with the phrase "after the sabbath" and to which "sabbath" does this refer? The Pharisees were the victors and it stands that way even today, however, neither opinion violates the date of the resurrection of Jesus.

The accepted view states that Jesus celebrated His last Passover with His disciples on the fourteenth of Nissan, which fell on a Thursday night that year. He was arrested and then faced the High Priest and the Romans throughout the night and early morning. He was finally placed on the cross around nine o'clock on Friday morning. He suffered until three o'clock that afternoon when He gave up His Spirit just before the Sabbath. His closest friends buried His body very quickly so that the Sabbath would not be defiled. At the proper time the women went to the tomb on the first day, Sunday, and found it open, Hallelujah! So according to Jewish figuring, the Lord was in the tomb for three days. First there was the part of Friday until sundown, then the sundown Friday until the sundown Saturday and the third day started after the sundown Saturday when He could have been raised from the dead at God's perfect timing. Would not the Father raise Him on that day which He had earlier named the *Early First Fruits?* I think so and so do many others!

We have all been taught that while Jesus was on the cross, His Father had to look away and that is why Jesus asks the question, "My God, My God, why hast thou forsaken me?" Many in the church believe that the Father forsook Him but nothing could be further from the truth. God never looked away; as Mary watched He carefully watched everything that was done to His beloved Son. The one and only reason that Jesus quoted the beginning line from the 22nd Psalm was to show any Jewish men who were in His hearing that He was indeed the Christ, the Messiah of God. Jewish men learned as boys each Psalm by memory and they were each identified not by numbers as we see them today, but by recalling the first lines. Read the entire Psalm, especially verse 24 to see that

Jesus was showing them that He was the One, the only One who could possibly fit this pattern and His father did not hide his face nor did He look away.

Shavuot, Latter First Fruits, Pentecost

Pentecost is the fourth appointed time of God and a Holy Convocation, which was fulfilled when the Holy Spirit of God came to live with men.

"And ye shall count unto you from the morrow after the sabbath, from the day that ye brought the sheaf of the wave offering; seven sabbaths shall be complete: Even unto the morrow after the seventh sabbath shall ye number fifty days; and ye shall offer a new meat offering unto the Lord. Ye shall bring out of your habitations two wave loaves of two tenth deals; they shall be of fine flour; they shall be baken with leaven; they are the firstfruits unto the Lord. And ye shall offer with the bread seven lambs without blemish of the first year, and one young bullock, and two rams: they shall be for a burnt offering unto the Lord, with their meat offering, and their drink offerings, even an offering made by fire, of sweet savour unto the Lord. Then ye shall sacrifice one kid of the goats for a sin offering, and two lambs of the first year for a sacrifice of peace offerings. And the priest shall wave them with the bread of the firstfruits for a wave offering before the Lord, with the two lambs: they shall be holy to the Lord for the priest. And ye shall proclaim on the selfsame day, that it may be an holy convocation unto you: ye shall do no servile work therein: it shall be a statute for ever in all your dwellings throughout your generations." (Leviticus 23:15-21).

According to Jewish tradition this is the anniversary of the wedding of God to His beloved Israel. Recall how He took her out of Egypt and how He took her through the Red Sea, a sort of mikvah. He then took her to His chosen wedding place and gave her a ketuba, which was and still is the traditional marriage contract in every Jewish wedding. Then God sent his request of marriage through His groomsman Moses to His chosen bride, and His Bride said, *All that the Lord has spoken we will do.*

Latter First Fruits was and is a time of harvest. It is also a grain festival. However, it is mostly recognized by the Jewish people as the anniversary on the day when God gave them the Law. It is remarkable to understand that fifty days after leaving Egypt, God gave the Hebrew children the Law. It is recorded that the first five Books of the Old Testament was called the Pentateuch. Today they are called the Torah. The Jewish Bible is called the Tanakh and it contains the first five Books of Moses, the Prophets, the twelve minor prophets, the writings which include the Psalms, the Proverbs and other books, which make up the Old Covenant work. They also have a small black Daily Prayer Book, which includes prayer for all occasions throughout the year.

The remarks of an unknown Jewish rabbi about this great gift are wonderful. A rabbi said, *The children of Israel were freed at the Exodus. However, they were not completely free until Mount Sinai.* He also said that, "Freedom without rules is anarchy." We certainly see a lot of that today as those who want to live without the laws of God or the laws of man produce chaos when they gather to disrupt the order of everyday business around the world.

In this harvest time within the regular animal sacrifices we see the addition by God of two loaves that have been baked with the new grain. However, there is the addition of leaven. This was a new offering to be waved before the Lord, and it was unlike all the other bread offerings. These loaves of bread for the first time represented the 12 Tribes of Israel and the gentile world. For the very first time God recognized us together in worship, because He knew of that day and He saw it in the future, the day when Jew and gentile would recognize Jesus. Thank you Lord! These loaves were both leavened because of the sin of us all, and they would be taken to the Temple and waved before God as a proclamation of the provision of God for all people.

There are strict traditions for this celebration. There was to be no servile work and the Torah is to be studied throughout the night. The Ten Commandments are to be recalled throughout the night, and the Psalms are read. They think that David, the apple of God's eye, was born and died on this date. The book of Ruth is often honored as is the marriage contract between God and Israel.

Now we look at the celebration of this special time from the New Testament point of view. Jesus was faithful to teach His disciples.

Here we recall the words of Jesus when He ascended unto heaven, He said, *"And, behold, I send the promise of my Father upon you: but tarry ye in the city of Jerusalem, until ye be endued with power from on high" (Luke 24:49).* And He also said; *"And, being assembled together with them, commanded them that they should not depart from Jerusalem, but wait for the promise of the Father, which, saith he, ye have heard of me" (Acts 1:4).*

Jesus knew that they would be at the Temple on that very date since it was one of the mandatory convocations; He knew they would be thanking God for the harvest, but He also knew that their thanks would grow even stronger when they recognized the great gift of the Law. It was now 1500 years after the Sinai experience and for all those years they had gone to the Temple as righteous Jewish men to give their offerings and to bless God for the harvest and their beloved Law.

Though there is disagreement as to exactly where the disciples were, scripture only states they were in an upper room. Most people believe that it must have been the room in which Jesus and His disciples shared the Passover meal, but that room is not large enough to hold the crowd that received the Holy Spirit. The Upper Room we see today when we visit has been changed a number of times so no one can be really sure. But if they met there it would have only been for a very short time for they were commanded to go to the Temple. Only the Temple would have had the space for the Holy Spirit to visit and then be able to baptize all the new believers. All of this was explained to us on our first trip to Israel. We were in the company of believers who had traveled to Israel with Zola Leavitt and we gathered to hear him talk about the room that the followers of Jesus might have been in. He concluded that it was not the upper room of the Seder meal, but it was indeed an upper room in the Temple.

Whatever the room, the arrival of the blessed Holy Spirit is really the most important fact. He came as it was written, *"And when the day of Pentecost was fully come, they were all with one accord in one place. And suddenly there came a sound from heaven as of a rushing mighty wind, and it filled all the house where they were sitting" (Acts 2:1-2).* Wherever they were there were 120 of them and they were waiting for God to move. As I understand it the number of 120 is the Biblical number of the end of all flesh and the beginning of life in the Spirit.

The description in Acts 2:1-2 is marvelous and exciting. Imagine the sound of the rushing wind at the arrival of the Holy Spirit, and how wonderfully He covered them with Himself. The name of the Holy Spirit in Hebrew is Ruach Ha Kodesh, and He gave languages of every kind to those who had received Him. I love to think of those who were from out of town; they were there because it was mandatory and though they looked forward to the trip and their time in the Temple, they could never have expected anything such as this. Imagine, these were men from all over the known world, who must have stood in awe to hear strangers and uneducated men speak in their own languages. What an amazing scene.

It is also interesting to note that these men had just been hearing a scripture written by Ezekiel while in the Temple, *"And I looked, and, behold, a whirlwind came out of the north, a great cloud, and a fire infolding itself, and a brightness was about it, and out of the midst thereof as the colour of amber, and out of the midst of the fire"* (Ezekiel 1:4).

The most important part of the moment was that for the first time in over 600 years, they were experiencing the Shekinah Glory from God. Hallelujah!

I have a prized possession, a copy of a painting about this particular period of time. On the right side is Mount Sinai with the fire up above and Moses holding up the tablets of Commandments while Jewish wanderers circled all around. There is a long train of them as they walk to the other side of the picture, which displays the Holy Temple of God, which is on fire, with the fire of the Holy Ghost. I love this picture for what it means with proof that God never loses us, never forgets a date and His timing is forever perfect!

God's Appointed Times, Unfulfilled

Rosh HaShanah, Feast of Trumpets

WE CALL THIS THE FEAST OF TRUMPETS, THE SPIRITUAL NEW YEAR. THIS IS AN UNFULFILLED SACRED ASSEMBLY, BUT COULD THIS BE THE SET TIME FOR THE CALLING AWAY OF THE CHURCH?

> *And the Lord spake unto Moses, saying, Speak unto the children of Israel, saying, In the seventh month, in the first day of the month, shall ye have a sabbath, a memorial of blowing of trumpets, an holy convocation. Ye shall do no servile work therein: but ye shall offer an offering made by fire unto the* LORD" (Leviticus 23:23-25).

Before we look at this particular appointed time, let us take a look at the month of Elul. Since this is the beginning of the time of the fall sacred assemblies and is quickly followed by a time of deep repentance during Yom Kippur, the rabbis have allowed this full month to prepare for that great Day of Atonement. They hold that the 40 day period from the first day of Elul, in August/September, through to the tenth day of Tishri, which is in September/October, was understood to be the period of time when Moses ascended upon Mount Sinai to receive the second tablets of the law and he descended on the day of Yom Kippur. This preparation is not just of a physical nature, but it is also very spiritual; and therefore, extra time is given. The entire month has been made available to those who are dedicated and ready to come before the Jewish God Melech Ha Olam, King of the Universe. Repentance for the Jew is a

serious matter centering on the renunciation of sin, the appeal for forgiveness, and the return to righteous living.

It would please the Lord if Christians would take this kind of time to prepare themselves so that they could stand clean and unashamed before our great King. *"Seek ye the LORD while He may be found, call ye upon him while he is near: Let the wicked forsake his way, and the unrighteous man his thoughts: and let him return unto the LORD, and he will have mercy upon him; and to our God, for he will abundantly pardon"* (Isaiah 55:6-7).

God wants His children to know that He is very near to us, especially during hard times.

We can ask for what we need, in particular ask for His peace and He will be faithful to give it to us. It is important to accept a simple statement, that if we are out of peace then we are out of God's will.

We must never forget that God has a perfect plan for each of us and whatever the problem, He will make the way. In truth, most of us know that God is near to us. We are the ones who distance ourselves from Him.

There are only ten days between Rosh HaShanah and Yom Kippur, which is the single most holy day of the Jewish year. Those days are called the Ten Days of Awe, so through the month of Elul along with the ten special days everyone should be able to settle their problems with God. Restitution for our sins is mandatory and through this time Jews take very good care of their personal inventory. And during the month of Elul the rabbis have prepared general lists to aid in the act of repentance. We must confess our sin and try never to repeat it. We must make an appeal for forgiveness and return to righteous living. The Jews teach correctly that repentance is not an emotion; it is a decision, an act of our will. Also everyone must be obedient to God. In accomplishing this, Jews must confess all their guilt, they must have remorse over their sins and resolve to never do them again, and they must be reconciled with God.

It would be good for us all to follow suit. How many times has the Word directed us to repent? Here are just a few: in Matthew 3:12. John the Baptist calls us to repentance. Also in Matthew 4:17 Jesus, called Yeshua by the Jews, called for repentance when He began to preach. In Mark 6:12, repent was the first word the disciples used when they were sent out, and in Luke 24:47, Jesus said it again after His resurrection. In Acts 2:38 Peter's instructions in his first sermon were to repent and again in Acts 17:30, Paul commanded repentance for all men. In Acts 26:20, Paul told the gentiles to repent; that's us and we better get busy because when the Lord calls us up we need to be pure before Him. Remember that repentance begins with God. Aside from God's grace, man is pretty much left to himself and we all know that man is incapable of finding repentance.

As we look at these scriptures let us not forget that old tried and true message, *"If it be possible, as much as lieth in you, live peaceably with all men" (Romans 12:18).* If we grasp its simple meaning, that means it is up to us. Only God can change a man's heart, but we are to walk in peace as much as we are able. And it is vastly important that we don't forget to pray for those who abuse and take advantage of us.

We have been talking about the repentance of the Jews, so let's take a moment to reflect upon our own relationships with the Jewish people. Have any of us ever had a difficult situation with any Jewish people? Have we ever held unforgiveness against them? And have we ever told evil stories about them, or is our thought life unpleasing to God? If we still hold bitterness in our hearts against the Jews, and if we have not as yet repented, this might be a very good time to take care of that situation. It is difficult, if not impossible, to walk a good

Christian walk with anti-Semitic feelings struggling in our souls. Always remember that our Lord Jesus was and still is Jewish. If we were wronged in a situation then ask for forgiveness and give it to God and let Him make it right. If we were the ones who were in error then confess, repent, and try to make restitution as God directs; this is the only solution. Either way we must give it to the Lord and He will direct our paths and then we will be returned to righteous living before Him.

Rosh HaShanah at the Temple and Synagogue Worship

The single most important part of the worship during this set time is the blowing of the shofar. Some people call this the blowing of the trumpet. There will be three entirely different shofar sounds. The first sound is called the Tekiah and that is one long blast. The next is the Shevarim, which is three short blasts. The final is called Teru'ah and that is nine staccato blasts. These blasts from the shofar are designed to sound like the deep groaning and sobbing of a repentant sinner. This series of sounds will be repeated through the temple or synagogue worship until all have experienced a total of one hundred shofar blasts for each day of Rosh HaShanah. The continuous blowing of the trumpet is intended to remind Israel about the merits of the beloved patriarchs and God's blessed covenant with Israel. It is also to confound satan who appears on that day to accuse Israel. It is a call to repentance for those who are asleep in their sin. The shofar is also used to call troops into battle so great care is taken that the call to repentance is not misunderstood as a call to war.

The single most significant purpose for this season is that the Jews believe that God opens the Books of Life and carefully looks through them. There are three books, the Book of Life for those who have been good, the Book of Death for those whom have been thoroughly evil, and the Intermediate Book, listing those whose sins may be atoned for at this time.

Most Jewish men wore white during Temple worship at Rosh HaShanah. Even today many men will wear white when they go to the synagogue since white is a symbol of God's purity and a recognition that all men need atonement. Even the blessed Ark of the Torah will be covered with white.

Rosh HaShanah is called the time of the *turning again* to God. It is a deep and penetrating look within us in order to repent of our sins and turn again to God. We look for the same thing here in America and around the world, a great returning to God. People who are tired of their evil and sinful ways and who turn to their Savior looking for His peace, will receive. During this time the rabbis help the people with some thoughtful questions. They ask questions such as, "How have we failed God, how have we failed others, and how have we failed ourselves?" These are very pointed questions and all mankind needs to take a look at their own lives and ask those same questions.

We will now look at some of the special traditions from the Temple service. Since this sacred assembly is called the Feast of Trumpets then we can reason that there will be plenty of trumpeting. During this time the Jews accepted that God was King of the Universe. They acknowledged again that God's intervention into the world was to punish the wicked and reward the good. They also recognize that God revealed Himself to them when He gave the Torah, and they recall at this time that God will fully reveal Himself again when He brings about the end of days. Also as it is written, *"He will turn again, he will have compassion upon us; he will subdue our iniquities; and thou wilt cast all their sins into the depths of the sea" (Micah 7:19).* Because of this scripture many Jews will go to a flowing body of water on the afternoon of the first day of Rosh HaShanah, and cast their sins away.

Their many traditions are carefully followed through this season. The Jews greet each other with a special blessing, in hopes that they would all have a *good year*. They also say, *May you be inscribed and sealed for a good life,* and the response usually is, *The same to you.* Many people visit the graves of their departed loved ones, especially those who have been very important to them. This is done with the hope that the departed will intercede on their behalf.

There are also certain penitent prayers that need to be said, and they recall the 13 attributes of God. These 13 attributes come from the scripture spoken to Moses by the Lord in Exodus 34:6-7, *"And the LORD passed by before him, and proclaimed, The LORD, The LORD God, merciful and gracious, longsuffering, and abundant in goodness and truth, Keeping mercy for thousands, forgiving iniquity and transgression and sin, and that will by no means clear the guilty; visiting the iniquity of the fathers upon the children, and upon the children's children, unto the third and to the fourth generation."* To repeat God's attributes... He is merciful, He is gracious, He is longsuffering, He is abundant in goodness, He is abundant in truth. He has mercy for thousands, forgives iniquity, forgives transgression, and forgives sin. By no means does He clear the guilty, and remember that He visits the iniquity of the fathers upon the children and upon the children's children, unto the third and fourth generations.

There are some delightful food customs through this season. My all time favorite is dipping sliced apples into honey before eating. This symbolizes the wish for a sweet new year ahead. During this season the Challah bread is shaped round as if it were a crown since the Jews recognize that God is King of the Universe. It is interesting to note that salt must not be added through this season. However, when fish is served the head is also eaten recognizing that the Jewish people are the head and not the tail. Some fruits are allowed, especially those which have not recently been tasted.

Additionally, they will eat no nuts through this time because the Hebrew word for nuts is *egoz* and that has the same numerical equivalent for the Hebrew word "sin".

This study in no way gives every detail and every practice of the set time of Rosh HaShanah. However, it does give enough information for the reader to get a clear understanding of the Jewish fall festival season.

Yom Kippur, the Day of Atonement

Could this be the day that all the Jews will be saved?

"And the LORD spake unto Moses, saying, Also on the tenth day of this seventh month there shall be a day of atonement: it shall be an holy convocation unto you; and ye shall afflict your souls, and offer an offering made by fire unto the LORD. And ye shall do no work in that same day: for it is a day of atonement, to make an atonement for you before the LORD your God. For whatsoever soul it be that shall not be afflicted in that same day, he shall be cut off from among his people. And whatsoever soul it be that doeth any work in that same day, the same soul will I destroy from among his people. Ye shall do no manner of work: it shall be a statute for ever throughout your generations in all your dwellings. It shall be unto you a sabbath of rest, and ye shall afflict your souls: in the ninth day of the month at even, from even unto even, shall ye celebrate your Sabbath (Leviticus 23:26-32).

To the Jewish people Yom Kippur is considered to be the single most holy day in the entire calendar year and it brings to a close the prescribed ten days of repentance, which are called the Ten Days of Awe. Also it is the only day of the year when Jews may receive God's forgiveness. Jews who are not particularly observant through the rest of the year will never fail to keep Yom Kippur. In the previous chapter we explained that at Rosh HaShanah, God opened the three Books of Life and it is at Yom Kippur that He closes them. Though the observance of this day has moved from the Temple to the synagogue, penitent Jews will spend

the entire day in prayer. For a Jew this is a serious time and all their ceremonies and sacrifices demonstrate the truth of that statement.

Yom Kippur Celebrations During the Temple Years

During the Temple years the observances were very interesting. The High Priest would be clothed all in white and he alone would officiate that day. He alone would kill the animal of sacrifice and he alone would bless the people. He would make atonement for the Tabernacle and the Altar. He would then make atonement for the Holy Sanctuary and for all the priests, as well as the people of the congregation.

It was understood that the High Priest made every offering, slayed every animal, and jetted the blood of the goat and the bullock into proper vessels. It was also very important that through this entire day not a drop of blood be spilled on him or on his spotless garments. Because of the strain of the specialized work for Yom Kippur, the High Priest usually moved into the Temple at least one week before Yom Kippur so he could practice moving quickly without making an error. It was a very full day.

A great number of sacrifices were made that day but the most interesting to us is the ceremony of the two goats. The story is told in Leviticus 16 and it involves two goats, which must not have been related but must have resembled each other in every detail. At the proper time the goats were placed before the High Priest with their backs toward the congregation and their faces toward the sanctuary. These goats would represent the sins of all of the people and a proper sacrifice. Two lots were drawn, one would be inscribed, *la Jehovah* and the other would be inscribed, *la azazel* which was the scapegoat. The Priest drew the lots from a special urn. He inserted both of his hands into the urn and when he withdrew his hands each one would contain a lot. He then placed one upon the head of each goat. The lots designated which goat was for God and which goat was for satan. It was considered very good luck if the lot which designated the goat for God was found in the right hand of the Priest.

When I heard that story I was reminded about the old days in Florida when those who gambled could play a game called Bolita. In this game there was a bag with many Bolita balls. Each ball had a number and those who bet would bet that the number they chose would be the number withdrawn from the bag. I once asked someone on the inside of this business how they could ensure that reaching into the bag to pull out the numbered ball that they would bring the one that would pay off the least amount of money. The answer was simply amazing. They calculate the least expensive losing number and put it on ice for a few hours. When the authorized person reached into the bag, he felt for the coldest one. Upon reading this story about the High Priest I wondered if the High Priests had a system of keeping God's lot cool.

Let us return to the goats. A piece of red cloth was now attached to the horn of the scapegoat, and a piece of red cloth was tied around the neck of the goat which was given to God. Then the High Priest entered the most Holy Place. The curtain, which was called the veil, was folded back and the High Priest stood alone in the gloom of this awesome place. During the days of the first Temple the presence of God was clearly visible as a cloud of His Shekinah Glory, which overshadowed the golden mercy seat. The mercy seat was made of solid gold and it sat upon the Ark overshadowing it. On each end of the mercy seat were solid gold cherubim, with their wings stretched out for protection. The Ark itself contained the two tablets of the Law, Aaron's budded rod and a golden pot of manna. The High Priest would then place the burning censer between the staves of the Ark.

I once heard a preacher compare the Ark of God to the burial place of Jesus. When we recall the Ark, we are reminded that there was a flat surface in the middle with cherubim at each end with their wings extended. Also in John 20:12, Mary first looked into the cave and saw the flat surface where they had laid the body of Jesus, then she saw two angels standing at each end. How wonderful that God never changes and the mercy seat once used by God for the Jews was then being used by God for the believers of Jesus. How awesome!!!

When we speak of the Temple we need to remember that in Herod's Temple there was no more visible presence of God so the Priest would place the censer upon the foundation stone of the Mercy Seat. Then the Priest would pour the incense into his hand carefully tossing them onto the hot coals of the censer. He would do this as far away from the glowing censer as possible. He would then wait until the smoke filled the chamber of the Holy of Holies.

Retreating backwards he prayed, "May it please thee, O Lord God, and the God of our fathers, that neither this day nor during this year that captivity come upon us. Yet, if captivity befalls us this day or this year, let it be to a place where the law is cultivated. May it please Thee, O Lord our God, and God of our fathers, that want come not upon us this year. But if wants visit us this day or this year, let it be due to the liberality of our charitable deeds." And on, and on, and on.

Finally the High Priest would emerge from the Holy of Holies and the people then knew that their offering had been accepted. Some might ask, how did they know that their offering had been accepted when the High Priest emerged from the sanctuary? The answer is simple, the High Priest was still alive.

Once more he would enter the most holy place to sprinkle the blood of the bullock on the foundation stone. Again he emerged from the holy place and he poured the remaining blood of the goat into the basin which held the blood of the bullock. The blood had been mixed so thoroughly that it was impossible to separate them. He then took this blood and sprinkled the most holy place, the veil, and the altar of incense and then he sprinkled the altar of the burnt offering. All was clean!

He came out from the Holy of Holies and he laid both of his hands on the head of the goat which was destined to bear the sins of the people and walk and die in the wilderness. He confessed and pleaded with God. "Ah, Jehovah, they have committed iniquity, they have transgressed, they have sinned. Thy people, the House of Israel, oh then Jehovah, cover over; I entreat Thee upon their iniquities, their transgressions, and their sin, which they have wickedly committed. Transgressing and sinning before Thee, Thy people the House of Israel, as it is written in the Law of Moses, Thy servant, saying, 'For this day shall it be covered, to make you clean from all your sins before Jehovah, ye shall be clean.'" The prostrated multitude worshiped when they heard the name of Jehovah. The High Priest turned to face them as he uttered the last words, "Ye shall be cleansed." In all of this the High Priest had declared absolution and remission for their sins.

Then the High Priest led the sin-burdened goat out through Solomon's Porch by an elevated walkway to the top of the Mount of Olives. There the goat was given over to a gentile to begin the walk to the wilderness. It is interesting to note that since this would have been the Sabbath then ten Gentile men had been hired for this job. They would walk half of a Sabbath day's walk and then hand the goat over to another Gentile who would walk another half of a Sabbath day's walk. This would continue until the goat reached its destination. A Sabbath day's walk was 1,225 yards by our measure. It would take all ten of the Gentile men to complete the venture and go the distance. When man and goat reached the designated area it would be on a projecting cliff. The Gentile would then tear the red cloth in half, leaving half on the goat's horn and placing the other half securely on the cliff. This would be a warning to any Jew who might pass by, that the scapegoat, which carried the sins of the nation, had been nearby. The gentile then pushed the goat over the cliff to his death.

Tradition says that if God accepted the sacrifice then the red cloth would become white as snow. We are told about that in Isaiah 1:18, *"Come now, and let us reason together, saith the LORD: though your sins be as scarlet, they shall be as white as snow; though they be red like crimson, they shall be as wool."* Now through a telegraph system of the waving of flags from place to place, the news spread that the atoning death of the hapless goat had been accomplished. Finally the children of Israel would receive their forgiveness. It is interesting to note that in Leviticus 16:21-22, *"And Aaron shall lay both his hands upon the head of the live goat, and confess over him all the iniquities of the children of Israel, and all their transgressions in all their sins, putting them upon the head of the goat, and shall send him away by the hand of a fit man into the wilderness: And the goat shall bear upon him all their iniquities unto a land not inhabited: and he shall let go the goat in the wilderness."* God called for the goat to be freed. After all, the entire goat really belonged to satan. Over the years many of these seemingly insignificant changes to God's original Word hardened the hearts of the Priests so that they no longer felt any guilt when they passed Jesus off to the Gentiles in order for Him to be killed.

They did not have enough courage to do the job themselves, but since they were accustomed to buying favor with foreigners to do their dirty work, this sort of perversion had become the norm. This is a perfect example of a lesson we need to learn because we often toy with interpretations of God's word to suit ourselves. In truth, under the Old Covenant, sin was never really blotted out. It was only set aside for another year or until the Messiah came. He not only took the burden of men's sins upon Himself but He blotted that sin out and purged it away. Each one of us who have received Jesus and His forgiveness know the deep sense of peace when our sins are totally forgiven.

Now back to the Temple. The High Priest turned to enter the Court of the Women. He read scripture and repeated prayers. When this was completed he washed his hands and feet. He put off the linen garments and put on the golden vestments, once more washing his hands and feet. He appeared before the Jewish people as the Lord's anointed. Once again he sacrificed animals and saw to the burnt offering, especially to the burning of the innards of the bullock and the goat, whose blood was used to sprinkle on the Holy of Holies.

The High Priest then removed the golden vestments, washed his hands and feet and again donned the linen garments. He entered the most High Place for the fourth time on this special day. He removed the censer and the incense dish, which he had left earlier. Once he came out of the most High Place he washed his hands and feet and put off the linen garment which would never be worn again. Then, he put on the golden vestment and washed his hands and feet. He then burned the evening incense on the Golden Altar. He lit the lamps on the great candlestick which would serve the night watch. Again he washed his hands and feet, put off the golden vestment and finally he put on layman's dress. When he emerged from the Temple a most happy throng escorted him through the people on the streets of Jerusalem. This evening closed with a fine time of drinking and feasting by the happy and forgiven people of Israel.

It is interesting to learn that there are people today preparing for the reinstatement of the Temple. That would include, of course, the animal sacrifices. They have already reproduced the holy instruments, the holy vessels and the great lamp, which will be used by the future priests. They have created the priestly garments, the oils for burning in the great lamp and the incense for burning in the Holy of Holies. These people have everything reproduced and have even been searching for the necessary red heifer. Some are waiting for permission to build the temple or the arrival of the Messiah.

After the Destruction of the Temple...

As in the days of the Temple, Synagogues were all dressed in white. The great scroll was covered, the Ark was also covered and priestly garments were all in white. The full intent of the Atonement was that all Israel would be saved.

Yom Kippur is a time of fasting and many of the righteous will spend the entire night at the Synagogue, praying, repenting and studying the scriptures.

There is a special service for the releasing of vows made under duress. During the days of the Inquisition in the 1600s, the Spanish Catholic Church brutally punished Jews who would not turn from Judaism and yield to the tenants of the Roman Catholic Church. Since that time the rabbis have made a way for Jews to be released from any vows that were spoken out of fear if they no longer agreed with those principles of faith.

Because there was no longer a Temple, animal sacrifices were no longer a part of Jewish worship. Since some believe that atonement cannot be completed without the shedding of blood, the rabbis have made a way for replacement of the scapegoat by a live chicken. The chicken was twirled over the head of the repentant sinner and he asked God to allow the chicken sacrifice to be sanctified as a replacement for him. This activity never became too popular and few are willing to participate in this sort of replacement sacrifice. In this day and age penitent men whirl a small bag of coins around their heads while they speak prayers of repentance. When completed, the money will be given to the poor. This is all pretty shabby and a pitiful replacement for the Son of God who died and shed His blood as the only true and satisfactory atonement for the sins of all mankind.

Through this holy day there are three major services. The righteous will attend them all. They will spend the night and the following day humbled before the Lord their God with the recurring theme of the need for atonement. The final moments of this day of repentance are very solemn. The time now comes for God to close His Books, which will not open again until the next year. Jews believe that true and final judgment will come at the close of the final day of Yom Kippur and at the final blast from the shofar when each life is sealed, waiting for the coming year. It is interesting to note that at the closing moments of the last service the scriptures from Isaiah 61:1-3 are traditionally read. They begin, *"The Spirit of the Lord God is upon me; because the Lord hath anointed me to preach good tidings to the meek; he hath sent me to bind up the brokenhearted, to proclaim liberty to the captives, and the opening of the prison to them that are bound; To proclaim the acceptable year of the Lord, and the day of vengeance of our God; to comfort all that mourn; To appoint upon them that mourn in Zion, to give unto them beauty for ashes, the oil of joy for mourning, the garment of praise for the spirit of heaviness; that they might be called trees of righteousness, the planting of the* LORD, *that he might be glorified."* The question that we ask is of whom is that scripture speaking? It is Jesus the Son of the Living God. They read the entire chapter looking for Elijah to come and tell them about the arrival of the Messiah, but He has already come.

I knew a Jewish man who was a student of the Christian faith. He spoke about the return of Christ and when Christ came he would ask Him if this was his first trip. There have been so many questions asked about the Isaiah 61 scripture that it has been changed and now they use Isaiah 58:1 which begins, *"Cry aloud, spare not, lift up thy voice like a trumpet, and shew my people their transgression, and the house of Jacob their sins."* It is not quite the same is it?

Also in Luke 4:16-22, Jesus Himself read the New Testament version of the Isaiah 61 passage when he delivered that stunning announcement that He was the anointed One, who would set the captives free. Some classic rabbis believe that these will be the very first words that the Messiah speaks when He comes. This fact has led some rabbis to speculate that the Messiah will appear on a very special Yom Kippur, which will fall in the year of Jubilee. They believe that the world will endure not less than eighty-five Jubilees and in the last Jubilee the Messiah will come.

The Jubilee was written about in Leviticus 25:1 and this whole chapter teaches us that the Jubilee is a year of emancipation and restoration. The Jubilee is to be kept every fifty years and it was to be proclaimed by the blasts of trumpets throughout the land. During the time of Jubilee the fields are to be left untilled, Hebrew slaves are to be set free, and all of the land and houses in the open country or in unwalled towns that had been sold, are now to revert to their former owners, or heirs.

Let us look at some of the prophetic scriptures describing the fulfillment of Yom Kippur:

Romans 11:7-10 *"What then? Israel hath not obtained that which he seeketh for; but the election hath obtained it, and the rest were blinded. (According as it is written, God hath given them the spirit of slumber, eyes that they should not see, and ears that they should not hear;) unto this day. And David saith, Let their table be made a snare, and a trap, and a stumblingblock, and a recompence unto them: Let their eyes be darkened, that they may not see, and bow down their back always."*

Romans 11:25-27 *"For I would not, brethren, that ye should be ignorant of this mystery, lest ye should be wise in your own conceits; that blindness in part is happened to Israel, until the fulness of the Gentiles be come in. And so all Israel shall be saved: as it is written, There shall come out of Sion the Deliverer, and shall turn away ungodliness from Jacob: For this is my covenant unto them, when I shall take away their sins."*

Matthew 20:6-16 *"And about the eleventh hour he went out, and found others standing idle, and saith unto them, Why stand ye here all the day idle? They say unto him, Because no man hath hired us. He saith unto them, Go ye also into the vineyard; and whatsoever is right, that shall ye receive. So when even was come, the lord of the vineyard saith unto his steward, Call the labourers, and give them their hire, beginning from the last unto the first. And when they came that were hired about the eleventh hour, they received every man a penny. But when the first came, they supposed that they should have received more; and they likewise received every man a penny. And when they had received it, they murmured against the goodman of the house, Saying, These last have wrought but one hour, and thou hast made them equal unto us, which have borne the burden and heat of the day. But he answered one of them, and said, Friend, I do thee no wrong: didst not thou agree with me for a penny? Take that thine is, and go thy way: I will give unto this last, even as unto thee. Is it not lawful* for me to do what I will with mine own? Is thine eye evil, because I am good? So the last shall be first, and the first last: for many be called, but few chosen."

Mark 10:31 "But many that are first shall be last; and the last first."

Zechariah 12:10-13 "And I will pour upon the house of David, and upon the inhabitants of Jerusalem, the spirit of grace and of supplications: and they shall look upon me whom they have pierced, and they shall mourn for him, as one mourneth for his only son, and shall be in bitterness for him, as one that is in bitterness for his firstborn."

Zechariah 13:1 "In that day there shall be a fountain opened to the house of David and to the inhabitants of Jerusalem for sin and for uncleanness."

Sukkot, the Feast of Tabernacles

"And the Lord spake unto Moses, saying, Speak unto the children of Israel, saying, The fifteenth day of this seventh month shall be the feast of tabernacles for seven days unto the Lord. On the first day shall be an holy convocation: ye shall do no servile work therein. Seven days ye shall offer an offering made by fire unto the Lord: on the eighth day shall be an holy convocation unto you; and ye shall offer an offering made by fire unto the Lord: it is a solemn assembly; and ye shall do no servile work therein. These are the feasts of the Lord, which ye shall proclaim to be holy convocations, to offer an offering made by fire unto the Lord, a burnt offering, and a meat offering, a sacrifice, and drink offerings, every thing upon his day: Beside the sabbaths of the Lord, and beside your gifts, and beside all your vows, and beside all your freewill offerings, which ye give unto the Lord. Also in the fifteenth day of the seventh month, when ye have gathered in the fruit of the land, ye shall keep a feast unto the Lord seven days: on the first day shall be a sabbath, and on the eighth day shall be a sabbath. And ye shall take you on the first day the boughs of goodly trees, branches of palm trees, and the boughs of thick trees, and willows of the brook; and ye shall rejoice before the Lord your God seven days. And ye shall keep it a feast unto the Lord seven days in the year. It shall be a statute for ever in your generations: ye shall celebrate it in the seventh month. Ye shall dwell in booths seven days; all that are Israelites born shall dwell in booths: That your generations may know that I made the children of Israel to dwell in booths, when I brought them out of the land of Egypt: I am the Lord your God" (Leviticus 23:33-43).

Sukkot is the third mandatory pilgrimage festival. The first is Passover and the second is Pentecost and those Jews who are able are faithful to return to the Promised Land and be obedient in worshiping their God.

Sukkot is the time of the fall harvest and it prepares the Jews for their time of winter. It is the harbinger of blessed rain. This season also finally lifts the somber mood from the season of repentance and judgment. Now we have come to a festive holiday, which is full of gladness and rejoicing.

The single most important part of this celebration is the building of our Sukkot, which many people call *booths*. There are three major rules about our booth; we must basically live in our booth. And for seven days it must be considered as our permanent though temporary home, and our home is to be used and considered as a temporary structure. The roof of our booth must be made out of natural branches, which will be covered with plant material. The general idea is to get more shade than sun but not so much as to cover the stars. This is a time to recollect and remember the many years that the early sojourners from Egypt spent in the wilderness. Decorating is encouraged using natural things, such as nuts, fruits, vegetables, carpets and chairs with tables. People are permitted to hang pictures and the children can make drawings, paintings and colorful paper chains. The family uses the booth for eating, resting, and telling tales of the old times together. However, it is a religious holiday.

There are special rituals during this season. For example, on the first night they light the Sukkot candles and recite, "Praised are You, Lord Our God, King of the Universe, Who has sanctified us through His commandments, commanding us to light the festival lights." Then they will recite, "Praised are You, Lord our God, Ruler of the Universe, for keeping us in life, for sustaining us, and for helping us to reach this moment."

There are special blessings for time in the Sukkot, "Praised are You, Lord our God, King of the Universe, Who has sanctified us through His Commandments, commanding us to live in a Sukkot." There is a custom of inviting special guests into the booth, such as angels, patriarchs, and any other symbolic guests they choose. A decorated chair is set aside for them to use, much as they do when they set a special place for Elijah at the Passover Seder.

There are also special commandments for this specific time and one of the most interesting is the gathering of the four species. This is a mixture of three branches...a palm branch, a leafy tree branch and finally a willow...which are bound together in a holder made from a palm leaf. Once this is fashioned together it is called a lulav and it is used to worship the Lord. When it is properly formed together, the palm branch will be in the center, the two willows will be on the left and the three myrtle branches will be on the right. The other instrument that is used alongside the lulav is the etrog. The etrog is a wonderful looking fruit that is similar to a large yellowish grapefruit in appearance and has a very good taste. Some used to say that the etrog is really the fruit that was eaten by Adam and Eve. *"And when the woman saw that the tree was good for food, and that it was pleasant to the eyes, and a tree to be desired to make one wise, she took of the fruit thereof, and did eat, and gave also unto her husband with her; and he did eat"* (Genesis 3:6). The reason many believe that this is the fruit that the original family ate is because both the wood and the fruit were good to taste and healthy for anyone. Good cooks will recognize the etrog as the original form of the candied fruit called citron.

According to some rabbis the four species symbolize four types of Jews. The etrog has good taste and a wonderful fragrance so they believe that this stands for Jews who have much learning and are noted for their good deeds. The palm tree has some taste but absolutely no fragrance. These are like Jews who do show learning, but lack in the good deed department. The myrtle has some fragrance but very little taste, which would be like the Jews who show good deeds but have a lack of learning. And finally, the willow which lacks taste or aroma, demonstrates a Jew who is neither good nor learned. The rabbis say it is impossible to destroy the last group so God has put them all together to atone for each other.

In the days of the Temple the Torah was removed from the Ark and held aloft. While the Torah is out of the Ark, the door to the Ark was left open. The priest stood on the Bima, which was a place that was high and lifted up. Then he held the Torah aloft. This was the place from where the Torah was read and sermons were given. The word was always kept high and lifted up whether it was being carried through the congregation or carefully closed into the Ark.

This practice is still followed in synagogues today all over the world. The message and the word are lifted up. During the synagogue service each day begins with the *Hoshana or Hosheaunu,* which means, *save us.* As they sing, they make a circuit of the synagogue just as they did during the days of the great Temple. Then the leader takes the lulav and the etrog and chants the *Hosh a Na* service and the congregation repeats every line. Those who have brought their lulavs and their etrogs proceed behind the leader as he circles the synagogue. Once they have completed the circuit of the synagogue and returned to their places there is a final hymn and the Torah is returned to the Ark which is then closed.

The message at Sukkot reminds the Jewish people that there is no real security except in God. He is their only hope. They spent their time away from their homes in makeshift booths and the instruments with which they worshiped were also of a very temporary nature; they can spoil very easily.

Great care is taken to protect the lulav and the etrog through the Sukkot season.

During the days of the Second Temple there was a very special ceremony which was called the *water service*. It was elaborate and joyous. As during Passover and Pentecost the altar of the burnt offerings was cleansed during the night watch at Sukkot. While the morning sacrifice was being prepared a priest being accompanied by a happy and joyous crowd made his way down to the pool of Siloam. He drew two pints of water into a golden pitcher.

At the same time another group proceeded to a place in the Kidron Valley to cut willow branches. Once they arrived at the Temple they would beat the willows against the three sides of the altar. When they had completed that mission they then formed a leafy canopy over the altar.

Then it was time for the priest who had collected the water to appear. He entered the Temple through the Water Gate, hence the name, whereupon he and his happy revelers were greeted with three strong blasts from the Temple trumpeters. The priest then walked over to a small rise in the altar and stood before two silver basins that were built into this part of the altar. There were silver pipes that directed the flow to the base of the altar. The priest then carefully poured the drink offering from the pool of Siloam into one basin. At the same time, he poured wine into the other basin. They were poured absolutely simultaneously.

I am always so touched when I read this small bit of history because the scourging of the altar is so reminiscent of the beating of Jesus and then the water and blood which poured simultaneously out of His heart for us. How wonderful that through this time of the year the altar of burnt offering identifies the sacrifice of our beloved Lord.

As this happened the crowd at the Temple shouted, "O give thanks to the Lord, O work now thy salvation, Jehovah." This wonderful holy moment was considered by many to be the highlight of the holiday service. Responses of the people were so filled with joy that they could be heard for many miles through Jerusalem. Many said that those who had not participated in this service could not know real joy.

Though they kept their hearts upon God's salvation the priest also used the scriptures as a prayer for rain. The priests would lead them in singing, *"Therefore with joy shall ye draw water out of the wells of salvation" (Isaiah 12:3).* Notice how they cried out for both salvation and rain.

Rain is a precious commodity in Israel. I would like to share a story about a precious moment during one of our wonderful trips to Israel. When my husband Bill was alive we were traveling with the members of our small home church. We arrived just after the Feast of Tabernacles and Israel's land was very dry. There had been no rain, which traditionally came during the celebration of this feast. Our guide was concerned because the country was in a state of drought and no sign of rain had been in sight; rain was desperately needed.

When we arrived at Cesarea Phillipi we disembarked and had a few moments of personal reflection and prayer. The location is very interesting since it is the very small beginning of the Jordan River. This river comes out from under Mount Hermon. That brings to mind many scriptural descriptions about its peaks and its feet, and the dew from Mount Hermon. We stood at that very time at the great mountain's feet and saw the beginning of the Jordan River. A small boy with a minnow net would have had a wonderful day except that

Israeli law protects all of these little fish. These little fish will one day swim on to the Jordan River and then on to the Sea of Galilee.

In this area there is also a very large red rock. It appeared to be about six stories high and the Romans had opened a large cave into the front of this rock. In that opening that they had carved and installed a statue of their little god Pan. In those days this area was called Pania. Today this location is a public park and is called Bania.

All of this is told so that each reader can understand the background and location that Jesus used when He asked His disciples a most important question. *"When Jesus came into the coasts of Caesarea Philippi, he asked his disciples, saying, Whom do men say that I the Son of man am? And they said, Some say that thou art John the Baptist: some, Elias; and others, Jeremias, or one of the prophets. He saith unto them, But whom say ye that I am? And Simon Peter answered and said, Thou art the Christ, the Son of the living God. And Jesus answered and said unto him, Blessed art thou, Simon Barjona: for flesh and blood hath not revealed it unto thee, but my Father which is in heaven. And I say also unto thee, That thou art Peter, and upon this rock I will build my church; and the gates of hell shall not prevail against it. And I will give unto thee the keys of the kingdom of heaven: and whatsoever thou shalt bind on earth shall be bound in heaven: and whatsoever thou shalt loose on earth shall be loosed in heaven"* (Matthew 16:13-19).

Some think that Jesus foretold Peter that he, Peter, would be the founder and builder of His church. Peter's name in Greek was Cephas, which was interpreted to mean rock, and many believed that Jesus meant upon that rock He would build His church. Some even felt as if the large rock in this location was to be the beginning of His church. In deference to all of those who believe this way let me state that all of these opinions were wrong then and are still wrong today. Jesus did not speak about their natural surroundings. He was speaking about the revelation that Peter had received from God that Jesus was His Son. The Church of our Lord Jesus the Christ, the anointed one, is built upon the two truths mentioned in that scripture. The first is that Jesus was indeed the Christ of God, and the second is that God will give His church revelation about all truth. Upon these truths His church will be built.

Now back to the special moment in this location of Israel. We enjoyed the area but we could see the harsh evidence of severe drought. All of the water in Israel comes from the highest peaks of the mountains and falls down the ravines into the major rivers, Jordan being the prime one. Water levels were obviously low; even those little fish troughs that we had enjoyed were very low. Israel is an extremely dry nation that usually received its best water supply during the Season of Tabernacles, but that season was over and so far nothing had come. We now gathered together and began to worship and praise Him, and then we began a strenuous time of prayer.

After a moment the Lord told me to open my eyes. Great streaks of rain began splashing against that large dusty old red rock. It was a strange color, looking almost as if the rock were cut and bleeding. I could not help but think about the blood of Jesus as it fell against the dusty hilltop of Jerusalem and ran down her ravines. Please remember God used these ravines to set His name forever in Jerusalem. Pretty soon the rain began to pour down and we all got thoroughly soaked and rejoiced in it.

Our guide was stunned. He had asked us to pray, but I am sure that he never expected such a response. Though it continued to rain for the next few days it in no way complicated our travel; no one would have complained even if it had. We knew that God had given us the opportunity to pray for rain and He did all the rest. The prayers for rain by the people of Israel had been answered.

Many Bible scholars believe that the Feast of Tabernacles is truly the birth date of Jesus. Most say that He was born on the first day of the feast and circumcised on the eighth day, which would have been the day of the water drawing. They have pretty well proven that Jesus was not born in December. This was a date used by the pagans to celebrate the winter solstice just as Easter was given to us because it, too, fell on the time of the spring solstice. It was easier to accept the times of the pagans than it was to learn the seasons of God.

One of the reasons that scholars base their premise that Jesus was born during the Feast of Tabernacles is a good one. *"And the Word was made flesh, and dwelt among us, (and we beheld his glory, the glory as of the only begotten of the Father,) full of grace and truth" (John 1:14).* In that day the word *dwelt* meant tented, or Tabernacled. In that day the Jewish worshipers called out for salvation and God sent Jesus to live among them.

When Jesus was a baby he was taken into the Temple for circumcision. Simeon the priest saw Him and rejoiced. *"And, behold, there was a man in Jerusalem, whose name was Simeon; and the same man was just and devout, waiting for the consolation of Israel: and the Holy Ghost was upon him. And it was revealed unto him by the Holy Ghost, that he should not see death, before he had seen the Lord's Christ. And he came by the Spirit into the temple: and when the parents brought in the child Jesus, to do for him after the custom of the law, Then took he him up in his arms, and blessed God, and said, Lord, now lettest thou thy servant depart in peace, according to thy word: For mine eyes have seen thy salvation, Which thou hast prepared before the face of all people;" (Luke 2:25-31).*

"In the last day, that great day of the feast, Jesus stood and cried, saying, If any man thirst, let him come unto me, and drink. He that believeth in me, as the scripture hath said, out of his belly shall flow

rivers of living water. (But this spake he of the Spirit, which they that believe on him should receive: for the Holy Ghost was not yet given; because that Jesus was not yet glorified)" (John 7:37-39). Many believe that these words were spoken by Jesus at the time of the water service. He often used natural symbols to speak spiritual truths, just as He did when He and His disciples stood at the great red stone in Caesarea Phillipi.

At the close of the final evening of the great Feast of Tabernacles, the evening lamps were lit. Old used breeches or girdles had been fashioned into wicks for the many lights this final night. Every light was lit; every Temple court was bright with light. The men who had previously danced about the water-bearing priest, now lit torches and danced through the courts of the great Temple. They sang hymns as they danced out to the Eastern Gate, and then they turned to see the greatest spectacle in all Jerusalem. The entire Temple was aglow with brilliant light. This was called the Great Illumination and to many it brought back the memories of the Shekinah Glory. It is thought that this was the place and the night when Jesus spoke, *"Then spake Jesus again unto them, saying. I am the light of the world: he that followeth me shall not walk in darkness, but shall have the light of life" (John 8:12).* Of course the Pharisees disagreed with Jesus and the usual argument followed.

It has been observed that the two most important ceremonies, the pouring of the water and the lighting of the Temple were unusual. They were different from all the other ceremonies practiced throughout the year. Though the truth will be revealed when we have all knowledge, it surely seems to me that those two ceremonies would make beautiful birthday parties honoring the Lord.

All the Feasts of the Lord have their own particular lessons to teach. We have studied the Festivals from the springtime... the Passover, Unleavened Bread, Early First Fruits, and the

Weeks of Pentecost. Then we endure the long hot summer, which many believe represents the church age. Finally we come to Trumpets, Atonement, and the final celebration, Tabernacles. God's final goal has always been to establish His Kingdom on this Earth as has been written, *"And it shall come to pass, that every one that is left of all nations which came against Jerusalem shall even go up from year to year to worship the King, the LORD of hosts, and to keep the feast of tabernacles" (Zechariah 14:16).*

The Summation

*G*od by His awesome wisdom has from the beginning of the calling out from Egypt, exposed to His chosen people living pictures of His beloved Son Jesus. Carved into every appointed time and holy convocation can be found the likeness of the Messiah. Even to this day most Jews do not know Him and they fail to acknowledge that the Messiah has indeed already come. The great blessing is that some have acknowledged Him, and with great joy they draw their salvation from the deep wells of their blessed savior, the Son of the living God. As the church age comes to a close more and more sons and daughters of Abraham open their hearts and freely give themselves to Jesus. Hallelujah!

Unfortunately, some within the body of Christ have not been eager to accept the new Jewish believers and the wonders that their special knowledge can open to us. This brings great harm to the reputation of the church and brings ill upon the Lord's body. We are all His children and we need to stand and be counted in unity. One redeemed soul with the next standing together in perfect agreement, one hand holding the other. We must never lose sight of the fact that the church began with a Jewish Savior and the first communicants were Jewish. It was only because of their quarrels that Paul moved his ministry into the heathen world which opened the doors of faith to us. The Jews were the original body and we were blessed when we were grafted into that body by our newfound relationship with Jesus. Our time is growing short and it would behoove us all to ask God for His Wisdom so that His work will be finished in time.

It has been understood by many that God prepared the holy celebration days of His calendar to foretell

the future. There has been some acceptance that the spring festivals depict Jesus as the Passover lamb, the sinless bread, and the risen Lord. Unfortunately few have looked to the fall festivals in like manner. This book presents the truth that if God would use the spring celebrations to show Jesus, why would He not also use the fall? Of course He did. As with all Biblical holy days, there is a prophetic as well as historical meaning. In Rosh HaShanah it is the calling away of the church which some call the rapture. Yom Kippur shows the final salvation for the Jews, Sukkot, called Tabernacles understood to mean God dwelling in booths with His people, is now being recognized as likely the true birth date of Jesus.

I found this wonderful commentary in Barney Kasdan's book entitled, *God's Appointed Times*.

> "Many classical rabbis saw a connection between Rosh HaShanah, the holy day of regathering, and the Messiah who would be the agent of the regathering. For example, in a work in the eighth century C.E. we find the following commentary. "Messiah ben David (son of David), and Zerubable. Peace be unto him, will ascend the Mount of Olives. And Messiah will command Elijah to blow the shofar. The light of the six days of creation will return and be seen, the light of the moon will be like the light of the sun, and God will send full healing to all the sick of Israel. The second blast which Elijah will blow will make the dead rise, they will rise from the dust and each man will recognize his fellow man, and so will husband and wife, father and son, brother and brother. All will come to the Messiah from the four corners of the earth, from east and from west, from north and from south. The Children of Israel will fly off on the wings of angels and come to the Messiah..."

While the historical emphasis of the holy day is repentance, the prophetic theme looks to the future day when the full spiritual regathering will occur under the Messiah.

It is also interesting to note that the Jews use the symbols C.E. that means the Common Era instead of basing time upon the name of Jesus.

Many other classical rabbis recognize a connection between Rosh HaShanah as the holy day of regathering and that the Messiah will be the final agent of regathering. So do not look for Him to call us away in the winter months, the spring months or the summer months, He will only do this in the fall and during Rosh HaShanah.

There are those who will be quick to say that as scripture states, *"But of that day and hour knoweth no man, no, not the angels of heaven, but my Father only" (Matthew 24:36).* I agree that we do not as yet know the exact day or hour. However, for those who have sought His knowledge, especially for the old sages, they have learned with joy the proper seasons of time. They understand that God gave signs on His calendar to show the way. Revelation from God is a blessed gift and as the time draws near He will give more and more understanding to His children about coming events. It is important for the church to be prepared and it is also a high priority of the Lord that His church would not be caught unaware.

I pray for those who have spent the time reading this book will accept the truths found within its pages, and that every reader receive everything that God put in my heart to share. This is His book. He gave me the information and He called me to write. It is His heartfelt desire to teach and bless the Body of His Son in preparation for the great day of the calling away of His church.

I love you and pray for you, Jane.

The Final Chapter

Well beloved, we have looked at the history of Jewish weddings, the wedding of God and His Bride, the appointed times, both fulfilled and unfulfilled, and we finally come to the last chapter, the much-awaited wedding of the Lamb.

We know the scripture tells us that when the Church is caught away the first thing we will do is attend a Wedding Supper. This grand occasion will be held in heaven with Jesus as the perfect groom and we the church as His beloved bride. By now we know that the Jewish wedding is made up of the betrothal, the marriage, and even that special time called the "week". They must all precede the Marriage Supper. One must then wonder if the Marriage Supper is the first thing that we do when we reach Heaven, then when do the betrothal, the marriage and the "week" take place?

Beloved bride, it has been recorded that there is no marriage between a man and a woman in Heaven, as found in Matthew 22:30. So by the time the catching away comes each of us must be thoroughly prepared and ready to take the hand of our beloved Groom and sit with Him to enjoy the Wedding Supper as husband and wife. What does that mean? It means we must accept the responsibility and completed the commitment of betrothal, which some call the engagement. We will have well finished the days of preparation for the marriage, and finally the marriage itself. And even that special time, the "week" will be a regular part of our lifestyle before we are called away. All of this must be accomplished while we are yet here upon planet earth.

Again let us look at the betrothal. The groom makes his appearance and speaks to the father of his chosen. Remember, it was Joseph who called upon Mary's family, spoke to the father, likely offered a gift, and then made promises that he would protect and keep her even to the offering of all his possessions. Promises just like those of the ketuba. Once all of this was done, Mary's father took the family challis and poured their best wine into it. Joseph drank first and waited to see if Mary would come forth in agreement and drink. She did this and they were betrothed.

Then the time is at hand for the personal preparation for your wedding day. The more we study about our groom the better we will know Him. The time after the betrothal and before the wedding must not be wasted but spent in searching for a deeper understanding of our beloved Jesus. He gave His all for us and the least we can do is follow Him. We all know that when we fritter away our time in fruitless efforts then that is exactly what we will receive. When we sow wastefulness, we will reap the same. Our gifts and offerings will be fruitless with no real value to them. Unfortunately this part of our relationship with Jesus is all up to us. We will get only what we work for. We all know that the time is short so I pray that we will not waste it in carnal pursuits. This world is full of gifts with no real value; there are more offered every day. We must be very careful that our time be spent in the blessed pursuit of knowing Him.

Some of us cannot read the book Song of Solomon without a momentary blush. We of my generation are not really accustomed to that kind of literature written for the church. However, it must be clearly understood that the love between Jesus and His Bride is spiritual, not carnal. The earthly natural feelings between husband and wife are for procreation and these feelings will not be followed by Jesus and His Beloved. But let me say that the intimacy with Jesus are equally as passionate as those written about in that wonderful book. Now is not the time to be shy and bashful; it is the perfect time to yield everything to Him, holding nothing back.

For everyone who has read my book, *Amazing Grace for Widows*, the night of my marriage to Jesus is known. Having been a widow for two years, I sought solace. God arranged for me to spend a month in an awesome and special place. There the Lord showed me an upper room all made of glass, and told me that one day our marriage would take place there, in that upper room. This was not easy for me to accept because the shrouds of widowhood still covered me and I was not interested in marriage. Slowly but steadily I laid down all of the roles that Bill had played as my husband, I had done this many times before but this time there was a real feeling of finality. These things were lifted from me and I was being set free from Bill. Finally the moment came when I could honestly release Bill as my husband. I was ready. None of this comes easily. I had carefully protected my marriage against all foes and the unwrapping of the marriage covenant is difficult indeed.

We who are female speak easily about Jesus as husband but what about our male counterparts? I do not recall many men speaking with ease about their role of being a wife to Jesus. This is ahead for them and I pray that men begin teaching on this subject because when Jesus comes for us all, He will come for us all; we the church will be one. He sees no difference in nationality or gender. As it is written in Galatians 3:28 He will come for us all...male, female, Greek and Jew. So get ready, my brother, and be receptive when the call comes beckoning, "the bride of Christ".

My job is finished. I have shared all that I know that is truly pertinent concerning the upcoming marvelous events which will come to pass when Jesus comes for His Bride.

Personal Invitation

*H*ave you ever considered that when you partake of the Holy Communion, Jesus is indeed sharing Himself in a cup with you? He has already made the promises which have been proven as true; the New Testament is indeed His ketuba to those who believe. Jesus made promises that He will love you, honor you and keep you safely even unto the giving of His life for you. Jesus has already completed all the parts of the betrothal. The only part that is yet to be done is for you to tell Him that you accept His offer, and then sip from the cup. Hallelujah!

"When is the time for the wedding?" you ask. The only one who can answer that is indeed God, Himself. Do not ask prematurely, but wait until your spirit longs for Him as never before, and the thought of living another day without His demonstrations of love is unacceptable. Then boldly ask the Father if the time is right. Over the years you have shared your thoughts with God and you have freely asked Him for many things and He is well accustomed to the sound of your voice so it will not take very long for the Father to respond to you. If the answer is "Yes," then He will tell the Son that you are ready to become His Bride. Soon you will hear that wonderful voice calling your name. You will feel His arms come around you, and His breath will be upon your face. His tenderness will overtake you and you will yield unto Him and then you will indeed be His.

The "week", that special seven days that are privately spent with your new husband, is the final event that must be accomplished before you can attend the Marriage Supper of the Lamb. Once you are married to Him then all of the special times spent with Him will count. Whether it is only seven days or seven years the time spent privately with Jesus will continue to add up and eventually constitute the "week". Again that choice is yours. The more time you spend the more intimate your relationship will be. Fill your life with Him and His gift will be yours. Treasure your time together and His Blessings will overflow you.

Be ready, child of God because the time is indeed short. May the Lord bless you in all that you do and say through these most important days ahead!

Beloved,

For those who have read this book and approved of it will be found to be as the wise virgins, and will be much better prepared than those who have just laid it aside. My call is soon coming to set everything in order for the catching away of the faithful body of My Son. Stay true to the Word and seek My wisdom for the future and I will finish the fine work that has already begun in you. If you keep yourself pure, prepared and attentive then you will not miss the great trumpet sound, which will call you to fulfill My promised destiny.

Your Father

Resources

The Ancient Jewish Wedding …and the Return of Messiah for His Bride by Jamie Lash (Jewish Jewels), 1997

Bible History Old Testament by Alfred Edersheim (Hendrickson Publishers), 1994

Daily Life in the Time of Jesus (p. 130) by Henri Daniel-Rops (Servant Pubns), June 1981

Evangelical Dictionary of Theology, Editor Walter A. Elwell (Baker Pub Group), December 1991

God's Appointed Times by Barney Kasdan (Messianic Jewish Resources International), 1993

The Sabbath, Entering God's Rest by Barry and Steffi Rubin (Lederer Books, a division of Messianic Jewish Publisher), October 1998

The Source, by James A. Michener (Random House), 1965

The Temple its Ministries and Services by Alfred Eldersheim (Wm. C. Eerdmans Publishing Company)

About the Author

Jane Crosbie Wittbold was born in Canada, lived in South America, and returned to Canada to finish her secondary school education. She then moved to Florida to attend Rollins College, whereupon she met and married William John Wittbold. They lived together for many happy years, giving life to a daughter, Katherine, and a son named John. Life was good until the dark hand of alcohol took its toll upon them all. It was at her lowest point that she met God and soon led her husband as well into God's Kingdom.

When the time was right Jane and Bill opened ...*in the Name of Jesus Ministries* in Cocoa Beach, Florida. The power of God was present to heal, deliver and set the captives free. They worked together for seven years and Jane continued for another seven after Bill's departure for heaven. It was soon after becoming a widow that Jane visited with Dr. James Wesley Smith, of La Grange, Georgia. He had heard the instructions of the Lord to prepare her for ordination. It was arranged by men but directed and completed by the Holy Spirit.

She is the author of *Amazing Grace for Widows*. She now lives in Winter Park, Florida and attends Calvary Assembly Church. Her life is full and happy while Jesus still holds His role as husband in her life.

www.ingramcontent.com/pod-product-compliance
Lightning Source LLC
Chambersburg PA
CBHW030929090426
42737CB00007B/372